C000255344

Detailed Lima 37 012 seems to have strayed from its usual stomping ground of the West Highland Line. The 'Scottie Dog' logo of Eastfield depot gives the game away - the scenario is that it is on a diverted Motorail working.

Written & Photographed
By
Peter Marriott

From the publishers of
BRITISH RAILWAY MODELLING

Warners Group Publications Plc.,
The Maltings, West Street, Bourne, Lincolnshire PE10 9PH
Phone: 01778 391027 • Fax: 01778 425437

Introduction.

Model railways at its simplest - a short train makes its way round a circle of track.

There have been many books and magazine articles written on how to, for example, lay track, make buildings, build scenery, plan layouts and weather rolling stock. There is certainly a wealth of advice within the hobby! But many folks still leave the hobby and take up other pursuits. The purpose of this book is four fold:

- To make the hobby as attractive and enjoyable as possible.

- To provide some guidelines as to what products and projects will provide satisfaction.
- To show those returning to the hobby that this is a really good time to take up railway modelling again.
- To show why it has never been easier to make a good looking model railway layout.

This book is not targeted at 'rivet counters' (those in our hobby who enjoy the real details of railways) but is

for those who want to just enjoy most aspects of model railways. They would like to visit a model shop, see something that they like and bring it home for their layout. They like running trains but also seeing their layout expand and over time they want to improve their layout. We are not ashamed that this book will feature some sectional track – if this gets folks into the hobby and allows them to enjoy their model railway surely that is right for them.

Locomotives are available ready weathered today if you are a little worried about damaging your newly acquired model.

So what's in this book?

This book has three main themes:

- We have built three new model railway layouts especially for this book. The layouts use mainly 'off the shelf' products that enable one to put together a working model railway in a reasonable amount of time. Stage by stage photographs illustrate how we made these layouts. We mention the products used so if you like anything that you see you can obtain these products.

- Dotted throughout the book we have two page features discussing common railway modelling topics. These short sections are not comprehensive 'how to' guides but they are simply introductions. The appendix of suggested books at the end of the book may steer you to acquiring a book that has more on your favourite topics.

- Finally we illustrate various compact layouts built by the author Ian Futers over the last decade or so. These layouts use different track systems, different scenic methods and even different prototypes. They are included to show how compact basic layouts can be fun to make.

Research undertaken for this book

In addition to dabbling in model railways for the last three decades we have attended numerous model railway shows in the UK and overseas

An overall view of one of the three project layouts built for this book. The retaining wall is by Noch, the track is Peco and the building is a kit-bashed plastic kit from Pikestuff.

and have been an avid reader of everything model railways.

During the course of the last two years we have discussed trends and developments within the hobby with manufacturers in the UK, mainland Europe and the USA.

We have worked with private clients who have been mystified as to where to begin and demonstrated layout building techniques at major UK model railway shows. It was at one of these (at the Warley NEC show) that we realised that there is still a huge number of folks who would love to be active railway modellers but quite simply don't know what to do to take their first step in the hobby. The array of superb products that is available for purchase both inspire and confuse them. They do not know what to buy first!

Why do less railway modellers now join the hobby as boys or girls?

When I was a child in the 1950s and 1960s boys used to play with Lego, Dinky Toys, Meccano, Minic Motorways, Scalextric and train sets. It was quite the usual thing to discuss these with other lads at school.

Today model trains are up against a lot more competitive range of toys for children and teenagers such as Playstation, PC games, worldwide travel on budget airlines and generally staying 'cool'. The latest batch of teenagers do not see model trains as a viable hobby. The task of manufacturers is thus so much more difficult today. They have the 'model railways are uncool' hurdle to overcome!

Why do some railway modellers leave the hobby?

Some left off 'playing' with model railways because of the distractions of 'local' pursuits, finding the other sex, football, earning a living, rearing families and good old home maintenance.

But in addition to those reasons we have:
- the hobby had become frustrating for some because, for example, their locomotives stall on the points
- decent layouts may take up too much room in today's modest housing
- the prototype railway is now quite uninspiring
- model railway equipment is now viewed as rather expensive
- electronic gadgets might be perceived as much more 'fun' than model railways

What can be done to ensure that railway modellers stay in the hobby?

There are various reasons including:
- most of today's products are better than ever. They enable well running, superbly detailed ready-to-run trains to be run through scenery that looks good and is fun to make.
- a compact layout can offer as much operating enjoyment and satisfaction to its owner as a large layout.
- some parts of the prototype railway are still worthy of reproducing in miniature. Preserved railway lines offer excellent inspiration and are dotted over most of the UK. And do we need to confine our modelling sights within the shores of the UK?
- it is true that the prices of model railway equipment have increased of late but who can deny the increase in quality and much improved running characteristics?
- some manufacturers, for example Hornby's Railroad range and Bachmann's Junior range, now offer very competitively priced new products.
- and in the world of electronics we now have DCC operation and sound. Almost everyone I know (in and outside the hobby) who has listened to DCC sound is captivated by it.

This is a great time to enter the hobby, to stay in the hobby and to re-enter it. Enjoy railway modelling – it still is the best hobby around!

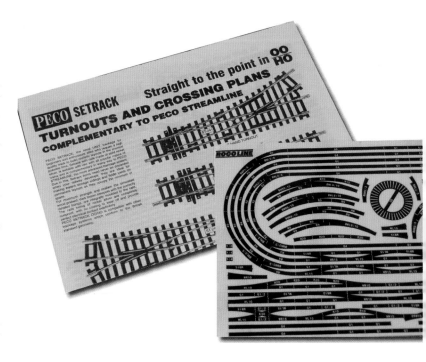

Track planning aids from Peco and Roco.

DETAILING A LAYOUT

A gentleman waits patiently for the next passenger service as the local goods train passes.

Road up! Bachmann Scenecraft figures provide the element of life here.

Various details add atmosphere to any station platform. Here Hornby's Skaledale range provides the lamp, seat, milk churns and wicker basket. The other items were taken from my 'spares box'.

- Do not try to be over ambitious when building a first layout. Rather than trying to reproduce Crewe or Exeter St Davids perhaps it is better to start with modelling a simple station.
- One's enthusiasm for a very large first project may become stale. Small may be better at least to begin with. Don't leave the hobby just because you become fed up with your first attempt!
- Anticipate that you will make some mistakes and learn from them. Mistakes are the best way to learn and to hone your skills.
- Do not be discouraged if you have to relay a point, fix a broken coupling on a wagon or repaint a building roof. This happens to us all. Patience is a virtue in model railway building!
- Model railway layout building is a multi-skill hobby. We cannot all become first class carpenters, permanent way men, miniature real

estate builders, landscape gardeners, etc, overnight. Use a first layout to find out what are your strengths and weaknesses.

- If you arrive at the conclusion that you will never be a good carpenter do not hesitate to call in the experts next time around. There are many small businesses offering well-built baseboards and legs to order. Some will lay track for you and build control panels too.
- Many track plans are based on a 6' x 4' baseboard which may look small on paper but in reality can be quite a handful. Have you tried moving a solid timber built baseboard single handedly?
- Before you decide on the size of your baseboards consider where they will be stored, how they will carried (and by whom!) and how will they be transported if you want to exhibit the layout.

- Does one need to model a station at all on one's first layout? Maybe it is better to use the first layout to test your track building and scenery making skills?
- Before you set foot in a model shop think carefully about which models you will use on a layout. There are huge arrays of tempting model products on offer today that could lead us into making purchases that do not fit into our overall modelling plan.
- Whilst some prefer to use just, say, GWR locomotives and rolling stock on a layout, others are comfortable using everything that takes their fancy.
- Think about how many hours and how much money you can spend on a layout. Both the cost and time commitment required for even a small layout can be rather surprising. If your budget is low be selective in your purchases. If the time available is limited keep your layout building sights down to seeing some progress within a reasonable period of time.
- Use sectional track to begin with to give you confidence at tracklaying. There will be no need to throw away this track if you do decide to move up to a flexible track system. The sectional track can be re-used in storage yards.
- Use some of the superb resin buildings to quickstart your first bit of layout real estate. They look jolly good indeed.
- Train sets and starter sets from many manufacturers offer an economical way into the hobby. Just check that you will be using all the components on a future layout to ensure that they offer the best value for money for you.
- Read magazines, books and ask questions at exhibitions to learn more about the hobby.

knowledge about a particular railway. Most societies have quarterly magazines that contain information about the prototype. It's a great way to meet like-minded enthusiasts.

- Enjoy the hobby! Don't let the little gremlins spoil your modelling fun. We all have times when a point sticks, one wagon derails and the sun has caused the gutters of your favourite station building to warp! You can soon fix most things in the hobby.

- Do not limit your research of the prototype to just the railway and its rolling stock. Look at general and railway architecture, signalling systems, scenery, types of trees, agricultural crops grown, breeds of animals, motor transport, etc. The scope for this research is vast but it will all contribute to the overall realism of any layout or diorama and add to the enjoyment of the hobby.

- Build a layout that has positive connections with you. That might be a past holiday or a childhood location. The more emotional connection with the real thing the more you will enjoy the layout building process.

- Relax – after all, it is just a hobby!

- Buy a selection of manufacturers catalogues. These contain information about their model ranges including locomotives, rolling stock and buildings. Some catalogues also feature photographs, diagrams, layouts and track plans that are inspirational.

- Spend a little time looking at Digital Command Control – it is the way forward for manufacturers and modellers. Listen to some sound chipped locomotives and look at the elements of control that are possible with DCC. Electronics need not put you off using a DCC system – it can be as simple or as complicated as you would like it to be.

- Decide at an early stage if you wish to use analog or digital control. In the long run it will be cheaper to use just one system rather than begin with analogue then change over to digital control.

- The value of joining a society of your chosen prototype should not be overlooked. Their annual subscriptions represent good value and help you to broaden your

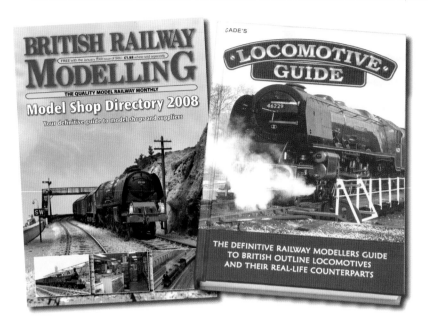

W here does one begin to find out more about the prototype and model railways?

- The first solution is to read all you can about the experiences of other model layout builders. Take out a magazine subscription and read about layout building on a regular basis.
- Choose to model a location and time period that really appeals to you. In that way you will go the extra mile when doing your research and making your model railway. It is not worth starting to build a diesel based layout just because someone gave you a Class 47 locomotive as a present when your real interest lies, for example, in the steam days of the LNER.
- Once you have decided on a particular railway company, time period and a location on which the layout is to be based, think about all opportunities of research. Some of us never get past this stage! These fellow enthusiasts are fondly known

as 'armchair modellers' who may be defined as one who enjoys reading about railways more than pursuing the practical steps of building a layout.

- The best way to undertake research of your chosen location is, of course, to visit the area or station. This may present a problem for those modelling a line that no longer exists or is some distance from home. But if your favoured location is within a scenic region, it may be possible to combine a family holiday with your research project. It is recommended that you speak to the other members of the family first!
- Video and DVD recordings are a valuable source of research material and a real boon to railway modellers. Many model shops retail pre-recorded productions providing good footage of numerous railways' historical and current operations. If you do not wish to purchase the recordings, local libraries usually

have a representative selection of local interest recordings available for hire. Some BBC television documentaries have featured overseas and British lines such as the *Great Train Journeys of the World* series.

- Even if you missed the days of steam on Britain's railways, visit preserved lines to study steam operations at first hand. In addition look out for the enamel signs on the platforms and other railway paraphernalia.
- Books about specific lines may be obtained from specialised book suppliers such as Midland Counties, Motor Books, Kevin Robertson and others.
- There are several second-hand book/magazine outlets that might have or will try to locate out of print material - see the advertisements in the railway press.
- Older magazines can be bought at a fraction of their cover price at preserved railways or at model railway exhibitions.
- Use museums as an important source of historical documents.
- The National Rail and Thomas Cook European and Overseas Timetables are updated regularly and are useful background information about current UK, European & Continental scheduled railway (and boat) passenger services. Reprints of historical timetables are available.
- Railway routes (current and past) can be studied using available railway atlases by Ian Allan and other publishers.
- Archive photographs can be obtained from Colour-Rail and other companies.
- Join a society of your chosen prototype to gain access to fellow

enthusiasts, a reference library, in-house magazines and sometimes even designated special interest exhibitions. Their annual subscriptions offer good value for money.

- Research should be as broad as possible. Include the railway and its rolling stock. Look at local, general and railway architecture. Study the signalling systems and look at the scenery, the types of trees, agricultural crops grown, road transport vehicles, etc, to make the picture as convincing as possible. Every detail will contribute to the overall realism of any layout.

- These avenues of research can be supplemented by visits to model railway exhibitions. Here you will find layouts that will inspire you, book dealers with magazines and books to further educate you and traders that will entice you with their wares.

- The Internet is a real boon to modellers. Type in the name of most prototype stations into a search engine and various photographs and articles will quickly become available. Many of us already wonder how on earth we lived without the Internet!

- The more you know about a railway company and its operations the more detail you'll be able to incorporate into your layout so hopefully the more you will be satisfied with the final result of your layout.

- Enjoy research but do not get too bogged down in it. It is just a means to an end.

Scratch-building, kit-bashing or ready-to-run – which is best for me?

In 2008 there is no need to scratch-build anything at all if you will be content to use ready-to-run locomotives, use built-up buildings and sectional track.

Only if you wish to reproduce a specific scene in miniature will there be any need to build anything from scratch.

Kit-bashing – using one or more kits in a way different to that intended by the manufacturer – is alive and well. It gives one's layout an individual touch.

If you are returning to the hobby after an absence of say 20 years, you will be amazed at how detailed today's rolling stock is and how well it runs.

This display of signs and locomotive numbers is at Buckfastleigh, South Devon Railway.

The fundamental part of every layout is its trackwork.

G ood track laying contributes not only to the realism of any layout, but also to the enjoyment of the models as they wind their way around the track.

Poor track laying may leave the modeller wondering if this is the hobby for him (or her).

Track for model railways falls, in general terms, into three categories:

- Ready-to-lay track sold in rigid sections or pieces. These sectional pieces include straight sections, curved sections, cross-overs, level crossings and points.
- Next there is flexible track that can be bent to the required shape. In addition there are ranges of points

(either in isolated electrical format or not) to match the flexible track.
- Thirdly there is hand-made track that uses a variety of relatively specialist components including real wood miniature sleepers.

It is recommended that beginners start by using sectional track. It's easy to lay and offers a quick way to get trains running in a short period of time. In my experience model trains work well on it too.

Sectional track

Both Hornby and Bachmann retail their own OO scale sectional track systems. Train sets usually come complete with some track – this may

be an oval of track, with or without a siding. The track supplied with the train sets can be expanded by track packs or by adding any number of additional track pieces from the manufacturers' ranges.

Sectional track is well built and robust. Most sectional track pieces come complete with fitted rail joiners (fishplates).

Sectional track components are readily available from dealers and are competively priced. Peco also makes sectional track in various scales. Their ranges are expanded with more components from time to time. They retail boxed Setrack starter track sets in both N and OO/HO scales.

Peco Setrack can be combined with their Code 100 flexible track, which can be shaped to form gentle curves or simply to produce a long straight without the need to join sections of Setrack together.

The sectional track ranges are not limited to just the track – some manufacturers retail level crossings, inspection pits, buffer stops, uncoupling units, power connecting clips, track pins and foam ballast inlays for both plain track and points.

It is quite easy to use sectional pieces of track from different manufacturers interchangeably.

If the geometry of the layout does not permit a specific layout, bespoke pieces can be formed by cutting pieces of either sectional or flexible track to fit. To cut track it is necessary to use a sharp fine-toothed saw or a Xuron track cutter.

Most sectional track pieces have small prepared holes in the sleepers for fixing to the base material. Track pins can be then used to affix the track to the board. Use a small hammer for this job. If using foam underlay do not push the track down too far otherwise it will distort the rails and affect running of the trains.

In addition to the familiar ready to run track systems mentioned above there are many other track manufacturers from Europe and the USA offering a comprehensive range of track parts. These include Atlas, Fleischmann, Märklin, Piko, Roco, Tillig and Trix

Flexible track

Those who are setting out on a first layout may prefer the simplicity of the Setrack system, but if it is realism that you want flexible track maybe the preferred way forward. Flexible track will involve cutting of the one-yard and one-metre lengths. Flexible track can be mixed with sectional track, especially to make the longer straights.

In addition to its sectional pieces of track Hornby retail flexible and semi-flexible track.

The Peco Code 100 flexible track system is known as their Universal range. Lengths of track are sold with wooden or concrete sleepers with either nickel silver or brass rail. Insulated points (Insulfrog) include catch points, small and large radius Y points, small, medium and large radius points, a three-way medium point and curved double radius points. In addition the Peco Code 100 range features live frog points (Electrofrog), etc. The Code 100 range of track is known as "coarse" track because of the larger dimensions of the rails.

Peco Code 75 ('fine' scale) flexible track system features wooden sleepers, live frog points (Electrofrog) with a similar range to the Code 100 range. Most of the locomotives and rolling stock from the current Bachmann, Dapol, Heljan and Hornby OO scale ranges usually run on Code

75 track without any problems, but if you do have any older items of rolling stock that you wish to run, it may be better to use Code 100 track or re-wheel the item of rolling stock.

Whilst live frog points may offer better current collection for locomotives, in my recent experience the current breed of locomotives run superbly over insulated points because of multiple wheel current collection. It should be mentioned that live frog points do require more wiring than insulated ones – hence they are probably not advisable for the beginner, unless you enjoy the electrical side of the hobby.

Narrow gauge modellers are increasingly well catered for by manufacturers. For example metre gauge track for HO scale (known as HOm) is available from Bemo, Shinohara and Peco.

Some advice on track laying

Solid and level baseboards are essential as the basis for good track laying. Even superbly laid track is only as good as its underlying baseboard.

As mentioned above, if you are a newcomer to the hobby, use sectional track to begin with. It will work well and will give you track laying experience. When you are ready to move onto flexible or finescale track, the sectional pieces can be used again in hidden sidings.

Purchase one or more of the trackplan books. Both Hornby and Peco retail sectional track OO/HO planbooks. The track plans in these books range from basic circular layouts through to mainline multiple track layouts.

Peco produce paper templates of their track system range that enable you to see which pieces are needed to make up the layout. The templates can be used over and over again as you experiment with alternative pieces to build up your proposed layout.

Be cautious when using any adhesive or ballast near the point mechanism. If glue sets on the changing blades it may mean that the point is damaged permanently.

Use re-railers to place your locomotives on the track. Re-railers are usually made from plastic and slide into a piece of straight track. By

might be their largest radius curve. For curves larger than R6 it would usually be necessary to use flexible track to make larger radius curves.

Some manufacturers specify that their locomotives and rolling stock should use a minimum radius of a number of centimetres. For example Bachmann specify that their locomotives should use curves no smaller than R2. The instruction leaflet of locomotives is the place to find the suggested minimum radius of a particular locomotive.

Sharp curves will, of course, not look as out of place on a narrow gauge mountain line in Wales, but they will look out of place on a main line or a high-speed standard gauge line, such as on the Channel Tunnel Rail Link.

Be very careful that any 'S' bends on a layout use curves that are as large a radius as possible. The curves should ideally have a length of straight track between them. Carriages will not move gracefully through 'S' bends and it will be impossible to maintain the close coupling of the carriage connections.

placing a loco or carriage on the re-railer, it quickly and easily runs onto the rails. Both Peco and Hornby produce such an accessory.

You do not have to use point motors on a layout if the points are near at hand. But if you do fit point motors, it is always best to use the point motors that fit beneath the point rather than alongside it. That said, there are now rather discrete point motors that can be fitted above the baseboard which can be hidden by small buildings, greenery, etc. Both Fleischmann Profi-Track and Roco GeoLine track systems have built-in ballast to accommodate the point motors underneath the points as clip-in accessories.

It is best to use the largest radius curves on your layout that your space permits. The fewer overhangs that rolling stock has on the curves the more realistic it will look. The radius is the length of a line from the centre of the curve to its outer edge. Manufacturers retail a range of sectional curves so R1 will be their smallest radius curve, R6

Another Class 47, this time by Danish company Heljan. It was good for modern image modellers that this company entered the UK marketplace. The model feels chunky and the Cotswold Rail livery is distinctive.

Basic locomotive stabling point in OO scale.

In this part of the book we'll let the pictures and their captions provide most of the information. This demonstration layout is intended to depict several sidings in a city location that could play host to a basic locomotive depot. This type of layout might be suitable for a modeller who wants somewhere to run his growing locomotive fleet, but wishes to limit the size of a layout. The four points on the layout provide plenty of opportunity to move locomotives. The headshunts are long enough for a locomotive and a wagon to provide a little more shunting variety. More operational possibilities would have been possible by featuring

AIMS OF THE LAYOUT
- To build a compact layout using kits and ready-to-go materials from a variety of manufacturers
- To build a layout on one baseboard that will permit shunting activities for locomotives
- To represent a small locomotive depot anywhere in the UK in steam days, BR Blue days or the current scene

a run-round loop. The layout could easily be extended at either end.

The layout would also be suitable for someone dipping his toe into the world of DCC. He could use a compact layout such as this to experiment with DCC and as his fleet of decoder fitted locos expands, there would be room for up to at least four locos on the layout at any one time.

The high retaining wall at the rear of the layout sets the inner city scene for the yard. The exquisite yard lamps provide some modelled height to the project. Fences, static grass, some signs, a couple of trees, a few barrels and pallets and several figures supply the detailing on the layout. A Hornby Skaledale brick-built building provides

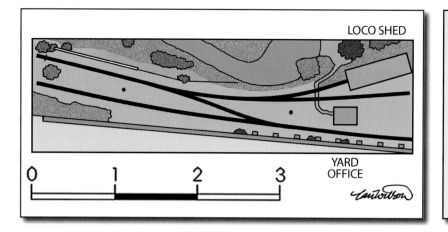

LOCO SHED

YARD
OFFICE

0   1   2   3

LAYOUT PROFILE
Size: 1.4 m x 0.8 m
(4'7¼" x 2'7½")
Country: UK
Location: Any city in the UK
Track: Peco Streamline
Control: Gaugemaster Combi
Scenics: Faller, Noch, Treemendus
and Woodland Scenics
Trees: Heki
Buildings: Pikestuff and Hornby

an easy way to represent the depot office.

Everything is available 'off the shelf' except for the loco depot building that was kit-bashed from a Pikestuff kit from USA.

On this layout I used Riko cork ballast. In hindsight it was only partially successful, as it did not provide sufficient depth to 'bury' the sleepers and running the trains is quite noisy, because the track was effectively glued to the MDF baseboard. I

could have sat the track on cork strip to reduce the noise level a little.

The layout took about 15 hours to build. It is quick to set up on shelves in the garage and trains can be running within minutes of wanting to 'play trains'.

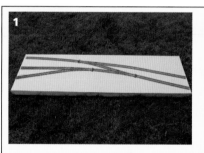

1. The baseboard has a 9mm piece of MDF for the top surface with a planed timber framework glued (PVA) and nailed to the MDF. The MDF was cut to size in store at B&Q.
2. The tools required for laying the track – a pair

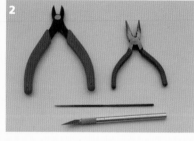

of Xuron track cutters, a small pair of pliers (for pushing the fishplates onto the cut rails), a small file (for finishing off the cut sections of rail) and a sharp craft knife (for cutting through the sleepers where there is an overlap at the points).

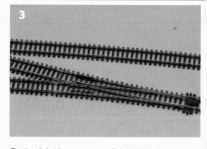

3. Track laid out on top of the MDF. The sections of track have been cut to size and have been tested by using a locomotive throughout the entire layout before the track is ballasted and fixed to the baseboard.

4. Ballasting equipment – an old coffee jar with RIKO cork ballast, PVA adhesive, a one inch paint brush for applying the adhesive to the baseboard and a pencil for marking the area to be painted with PVA.

5. A small pile of RIKO cork ballast shown next to a pencil for size comparison.
6. Ballasting, the first stage – PVA is spread in the marked area then the track is pushed into the glue and then the cork ballast is sprinkled

along the middle and edge of the track either by hand or through a sieve. Do not put any adhesive under the moving part of the point – just paint this section with acrylic paint.

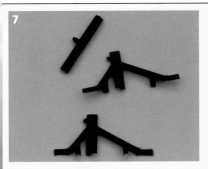

7. A Peco rail built buffer stop. The three parts are simple to assemble, just use contact adhesive and when dry, paint the buffer stop with matt acrylics highlighting the lamp.

8. The area next to the ballast was painted with brown acrylic paint. Between the tracks Treemendus earth mixture was laid on top of spread PVA to represent dirt.

9. What you'll see in the model shop - the packaging for the Hornby Skaledale Boiler House.

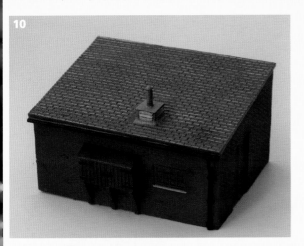

10. A Hornby Skaledale Boiler House was used as a depot office on the layout. I have found these resin buildings to be well finished and, to speed up the modelling process, they come fully assembled.

11. Security fence by 4D Model Shop. The fence needs to be carefully cut out from the fret using a sharp craft knife. We used several coats of well-stirred acrylic paint on the fence once it was firmly fixed to the baseboard.

12. Woodland Scenics Foliage that will be used to represent the creeping weeds along the retaining wall of the layout.

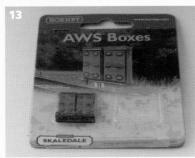

13. The Hornby AWS boxes come in packs of two.
14. Noch wall section. This layout required two of the Noch extra long sections. These walls are

made from hardfoam. They are lightweight and come ready painted with good relief and stone effect.

15. Two different pieces of Noch stone walling were fixed along the rear of the layout. We used PVA adhesive to fix the wall sections to the MDF baseboard and to each other.

16. Whilst the PVA fixing the two sections of walls together was drying a Woodlands Scenics T pin ('Foam Nail') was used to hold the sections together.

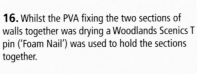

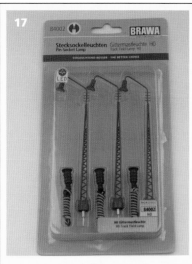

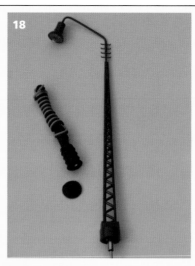

17. The two yard lights on the layout were by Brawa. These lights have LEDs and simply need to be pushed into the connector that fits into a hole drilled in the MDF baseboard.

18. A Brawa yard lamp with its connector. The rolled up wire goes underneath the baseboard.

19. The simple fitting instructions for the Brawa lights.

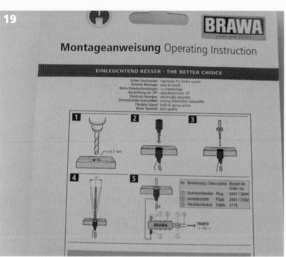

20. Faller iron railings are available for many railway-orientated locations. These locations include viaducts, bridges, in depots and alongside a road.

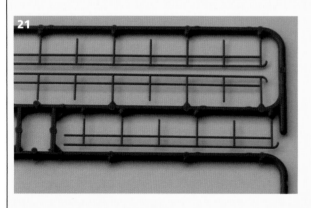

21. Faller iron railings as they appear in the box on the plastic sprues. The railings can easily be cut from the sprue with a sharp craft knife over a cutting board. The rails can either be painted on the sprue or once they have been finally positioned on the layout. All purpose adhesive or PVA can be used to fix them to the baseboard. Ensure that they are supported in an upright position whilst the adhesive dries.

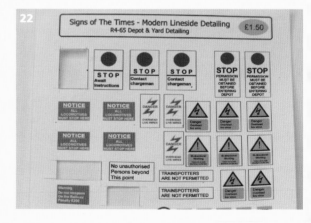

22. Railway signs around a depot or yard make a difference to the final appearance of a layout. In this case we used Signs of the Times notices. These were cut out from the backing sheet with a sharp craft knife. The post was made from a short length of plastic tube and the sign was fixed to the post using a dab of all-purpose adhesive.

23. The single road loco shed was made from a Pikestuff kit. These plastic kits from USA are imported by Model Junction (www. modeljunction.info) and other companies. The Pikestuff range is large and whilst it is made to HO scale, for OO layouts the kits are useful for modern and industrial structures. For more information about the range go to www. rixproducts.com.

24. Here are the parts of the Pikestuff one or two road locomotive shed kit (stock number 541-0008) as used on the layout.

25. Both ends of the Pikestuff building are marked so that it may be built with one or two doors. The side walls too have a selection of marked locations for doors or windows. It is the builder's choice which apertures are used – it is simply a matter of cutting out the chosen

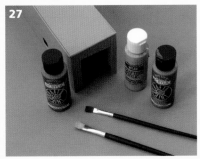

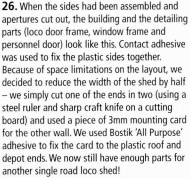

aperture on the reverse of the wall with a sharp craft knife.

26. When the sides had been assembled and apertures cut out, the building and the detailing parts (loco door frame, window frame and personnel door) look like this. Contact adhesive was used to fix the plastic sides together. Because of space limitations on the layout, we decided to reduce the width of the shed by half – we simply cut one of the ends in two (using a steel ruler and sharp craft knife on a cutting board) and used a piece of 3mm mounting card for the other wall. We used Bostik 'All Purpose' adhesive to fix the card to the plastic roof and depot ends. We now still have enough parts for another single road loco shed!

27. The loco shed was painted using flat brushes and a selection of acrylic paints. The sides and roof were painted before the window, door and doorframes were added.

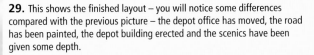

28. This picture shows the layout after the track has been ballasted and fixed to the baseboard. Some areas have simply been covered with green scenic material, the space for the road and car park has been left untouched, a couple of trees have been planted, the depot office has been 'planted' into the scene using PVA (though this was later moved) and the security fence has been fixed towards the rear of the scene.

29. This shows the finished layout – you will notice some differences compared with the previous picture – the depot office has moved, the road has been painted, the depot building erected and the scenics have been given some depth.

30. Two Lima Class 37s idling in the depot. This scene typifies a shed on the West Highland Line in the early 1990s.

31. Aerial view of the depot with Brawa yard lamp, Hornby Skaledale building, Woodland Scenics vegetation, figures by Preiser and Noch and earth texture by Treemendus.

32. Another view of the depot scene – the oil drums, palleted load and various items of yard paraphernalia add to the realism of the scene. All were attached to the layout with a dab of PVA.

33. A Bachmann Class 37/4 locomotive *Aluminium 100* visits the depot.

34. Diesel fuel oil arriving at the depot in a weathered tanker. The wagon is a Modelzone special edition by Bachmann. The figure is by Preiser.

35. A video photographer stands knee deep in static grass. The fence is by Faller, the photographer is a Noch figure, the sign is by Signs of The Times and the static grass is by Noch.

36. A visiting Class 47 bearing Great Western livery visits the depot – the locomotive was made by Lima.

37. A nicely turned out Lotus Cortina parked by the trackside. The model is by Oxford Diecast. There are a growing number of manufacturers offering miniature road vehicles. They are generally of good quality with

fitted flush glazing, interiors and excellent detail.
38. A little more shunting of the fuel oil in the yard.

39. Lima and Bachmann Class 37s meet at Brown Street Yard.

40. A vintage Hornby Class 47 – this model was detailed and repainted, though the silver wheels do give away its age.

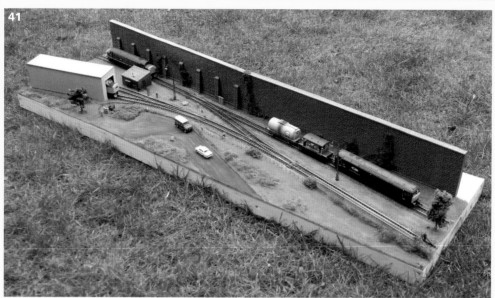

41. Another view of the entire layout.

42. *Aluminium 100* moves around the yard.

43. The Hornby Skaledale Boiler House was used on the layout as a depot office. Here it is shown in its original position on the layout. Once the depot building was fixed, it was realised that the depot office would restrict the view of the locomotives as they moved in and out of the shed so it was moved further back. This was simply done by pushing the blade of a fine screwdriver under a corner of the building and lifting it up slowly – even though the PVA had dried, lifting the building did not damage it. If PVA has set, it can be normally be released by applying a few drops of near-boiling water to it using an eyedropper.

44. The yard lamp is by Brawa, the security fence is by 4 D Model Shop, the retaining wall by Noch, the creeping foliage by Woodland Scenics and the leaves on the bushes in the middle ground by Noch.

45. The bush in the centre of the picture is simply a 'ball' of Woodland Scenics Poly Fibre fixed to the baseboard with PVA and then some Noch leaves (Laub) sprinkled on top of a little more PVA.

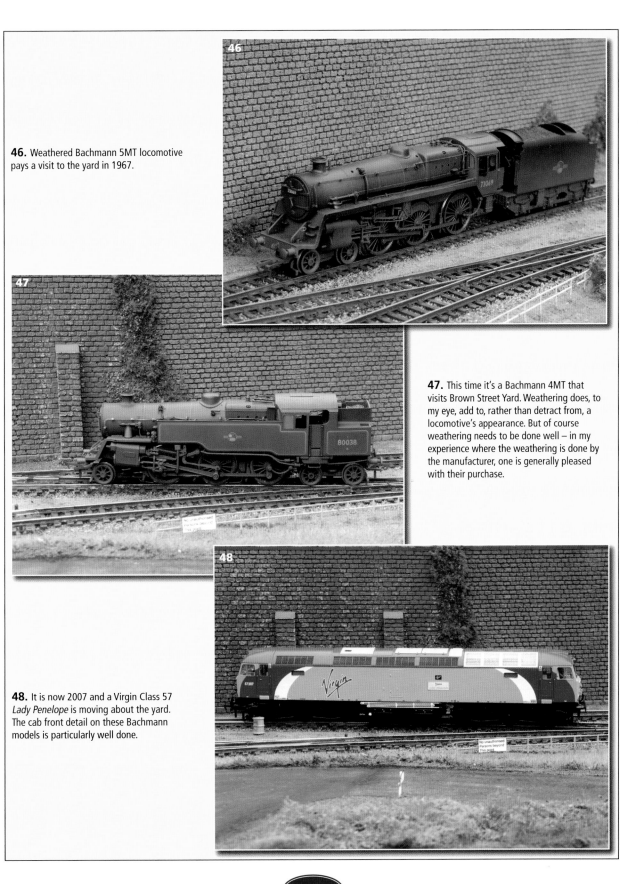

46. Weathered Bachmann 5MT locomotive pays a visit to the yard in 1967.

47. This time it's a Bachmann 4MT that visits Brown Street Yard. Weathering does, to my eye, add to, rather than detract from, a locomotive's appearance. But of course weathering needs to be done well – in my experience where the weathering is done by the manufacturer, one is generally pleased with their purchase.

48. It is now 2007 and a Virgin Class 57 *Lady Penelope* is moving about the yard. The cab front detail on these Bachmann models is particularly well done.

OLD AND NEW

Current day modellers have never had it so good!

Even model railway magazines are so much more visually attractive these days. In the 1980s the majority of the editorial pages featured black and white photographs.

This is the type of ready-built building that was familiar in the 1960s. Its plastic construction does not display too much realism, but at that time the choice of buildings for modellers was limited.

Back in the mid 1980s Dapol produced a model in OO scale of the J94 Austerity 0-6-0 tank locomotive. It was good for its day in terms of detail and running ability.

Hornby now produce a much improved version of the J94. Note the weathered finish of the locomotive and overall better appearance.

Today's modellers are fortunate - resin buildings straight out of the box look superb. Here is an OO scale station building from the Bachmann Scenecraft range, introduced in 2008.

In 2008 we are also well blessed with full colour magazines with detailed product reviews and descriptions of layouts. The design of modern magazines is attractive to the eye and informative.

Mainline Class 03 shunter awaiting the
consignment of wa●

Canal-side shunting layout.

The baseboard for this layout measures just 1.6m x 0.38m. This was the largest that I could comfortably fit into my then car, a Vauxhall Astra, with the rear seats down. Because I do not really enjoy baseboard connections I decided to make this layout in one piece. Though of compact proportions, as anyone who has tried to move a layout of this size on their own will know, it is still a little awkward going up and down stairs, etc.

AIMS OF THE LAYOUT
• To make a one baseboard layout that would fit into a small hatchback car
• To feature a relatively timeless scene that could be suitable for steam and the early diesel period
• To represent a canal-side location with warehouses

I built this layout some years ago and at that time wood insulation board was my favoured material for the baseboard top. I think that the layout was the last time I used that material, because it is definitely quite fragile in relation to pinning things to it. It would be unsuitable for a layout with catenary – the posts would not be strongly supported in this material. To support the baseboard top I used a frame of planed timber.

Detailed Lima Class 37 locomotives stand in front of the warehouses.

The track plan is a line running along the side of the canal, plus a run-round loop and two other sidings. Trains arrive on the layout from the off-scene sidings at the rear right-hand side of the layout. On this layout I used Fleischmann Profi-Track. It's simply a clip together ready-ballasted range with a good selection of track geometries and accessories. Point motors sit alongside the points in a discreet slim box that I hid with a little greenery. I have found this track to be easy to assemble, the joints are very close and robust with a fairly decent looking ballast effect, that is better once some weathering has been applied. The same goes for the Code

LAYOUT PROFILE

Size: 1.6 m x 0.38 m (5'3" x 1'3")
Country: UK
Location: Canal side, no definite location
Track: Fleischmann Profi ready ballasted
Control: Hammant & Morgan Clipper
Scenics: Heki and Woodland Scenics
Trees: K&M
Buildings: Ratio, Lima, Prototype Kits and scratch-built

Small details such as the signs do contribute to a more realistic looking layout.

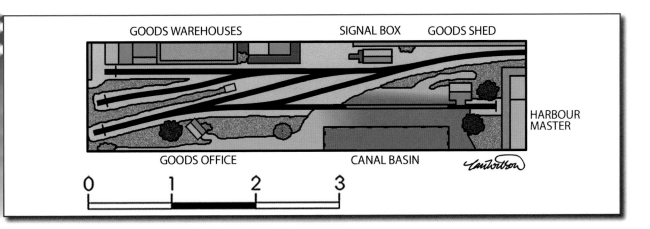

GOODS WAREHOUSES   SIGNAL BOX   GOODS SHED

HARBOUR MASTER

GOODS OFFICE   CANAL BASIN

0   1   2   3

Passenger services on the Wharf! A Lima Class 121 'Bubblecar' passes a Mainline Class 03 shunter.

100 rails. My one negative comment about the track is that it does give noisy running of the trains.

I used one of those faithful Hammant & Morgan 'Clipper' units – transformer and controller built in one.

Scenery and the details

This is one of the few layouts I've built that does not require a goodly amount of countryside!

All the ground on the baseboard is flat, taken up with sidings, roads, the wharf-side and a few areas with vegetation. To the rear and right-hand side of the baseboard are warehouses. Some were scratch-built using Superquick brick papers, Wills plastic sheets, Plastruct girders and Slater's lettering. The windows and doors were also by Wills. One of the warehouses was a paper kit given away in *Scale Model Trains* magazine.

A Dapol 0-4-0 'Pug' gives the layout a BR steam days look.

The style of the buildings is generic rather than specific.

There are three smaller buildings on the layout – a Ratio Provender Store, a permanent way hut by Prototype Kit (with Wills plastic sheet roofing) and a large signal cabin at the rear of the layout which was by Lima,

that I found in a sale bin at a model shop.

The undergrowth was mainly Woodland Scenics products. The trees were a mixture from various manufacturers – there were a couple of K&M large deciduous specimens and some others that I do not know

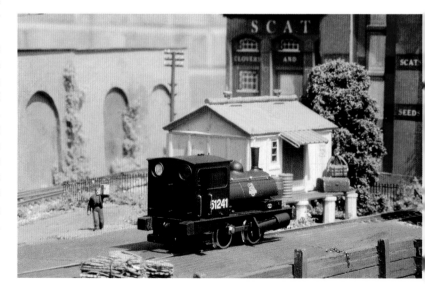

Dapol J94 tank shunts the wharf side siding.

who they were made by. The creepers on the walls and buildings were teased-out foliage mat by Heki.

Around the wharf-side, Wills timber sheets were used to represent the wharf. These were painted with acrylics and dry-brushed with light grey to highlight the grain effect.

Ratio fencing, telegraph poles by Airfix and a variety of loads and people were dotted around the layout from manufacturers including Noch, Merit, and Faller.

The sides of the canal were timber strips glued together with PVA. The water in the canal was painted with a variety of acrylics and then once the paint was dry two thin layers of varnish were poured on. I assembled a cardboard canal barge to sit in the base of the canal.

Layout under construction showing the spray painted timber strips used for the side of the canal with kit-built Ratio Provender Store ready to be inserted into the scene.

Below right: Inspiration for Peat's Wharf at Gloucester Docks.

Below left: Barge, warehouses and rail siding at Gloucester Docks .

Staverton Station, South Devon Railway.

Looking towards Buckfastleigh with level crossing and ground signal cabin.

Above: Tiny signal cabin at Staverton. Wills makes a plastic kit in OO scale that can be adapted to look similar to this cabin.

Right: Trolley full of classic luggage.

Private owner wagon in the siding at Staverton. There are a lot of available private owner wagons in both OO and N scales, in ready-to-run and kit form.

Milk churns are available ready painted in OO scale from Hornby Skaledale. Signs are available from Tiny Signs.

Platform seat and sign. The hobby is blessed with a lot of suppliers for these details such as Dart Castings, Ten Commandments and Langley Models.

This small goods shed would be an ideal first scratch-building project that could be made from card or plastic.

The scenery on any model railway transforms bare baseboards and track into a work of art; Making scenery is fun, it's artistic and even therapeutic! In 2008, we are blessed with many excellent products that help us to make scenery as simply and quickly as possible.

In this section we will summarise the main aspects of making the landscape, these techniques are suitable for most scales.

Stage-by-stage, scenery can be broken down into the following tasks:

- Hillsides, cuttings, embankments, and rocks faces all need good foundations. Plywood, MDF, hardboard and thick cardboard can all be used as formers for the contours of the scenery.
- Crumpled newspaper or wrapping from parcels can then be pushed between the formers to give support for the landscape. Alternative products for this support are chicken wire or polystyrene blocks that can be cut and shaped to produce the groundwork contours.
- To form the 'land' use plaster impregnated cloth that is available at most model shops under the name of Mod-Roc or Woodland Scenics' Plaster Cloth.
- Cut the plaster-impregnated cloth into hand-size sections and soak in a bowl of water for a few seconds. Then lay it across the top of the foundation material. The cloth will stay workable for a few minutes. Smooth down the cloth whilst it dries. This part of the scenery building process is the messiest! The cloth will be fully dry by the next day.
- When the cloth is dry, paint the entire landscape with the cheapest paint that you can find - preferably non-gloss brown, grey, black or green. Acrylics, poster colours, and household water-based emulsion paints may all be used.

- In my experience, it is best to then use two layers of scatter material to give depth and variety to the ground cover.
- When the paint is dry (usually after a few hours) cover the landscape with the first layer of scatter material by sprinkling it on brushed on PVA adhesive (white glue sold in plastic bottles of various sizes at all DIY shops) or Woodland Scenics' Scenic Glue. For the first layer, apply the cheapest scatter material you can buy. Save the better quality materials for the second coat.
- It is necessary to wait until the first coat fully dries before applying the second coat. If the board is portable shake off and keep any excess scatter materials.
- Re-coat the area with adhesive again and cover with better quality scatter materials such as Woodland Scenics Fine, Coarse or Underbrush Alternative products are by Auhagen Anita Décor, Heki, Hornby, Noch and others. Mix the colours and the textures – ground cover is never a consistent colour. Again remove the excess (when fully dry) and save it.
- To make rock faces, use proprietary products such as Heki landscape modelling clay or the Woodland Scenics Terrain System. Alternatively the more familiar products such as Polyfilla can be used. Noch make rock faces from hardfoam – it is easy to work with and light in weight.
- Add further texture to the completed grass banks, rock faces, etc. Dab a few spots of PVA glue, at random and dab on foam groundcover pieces bushes or lichen available from Woodland Scenics, Noch, Heki and others.
- Include taller grasses to add height to the scene – these are available from

Woodlands Scenics, Faller, Noch, Set Scenes, Treemendus and others.
- Use static grass by Noch and other companies to give that 3D effect.
- Plant a few trees. There are many good models of trees available today.
- Add fences, roads, animals, people and vehicles.
- And to finish, boil the kettle, stand back and admire your little piece of countryside!

This has been a very quick canter through the world of making scenery. There is a lot more to be said about water, rock faces, trees, undergrowth, roads, people, motor vehicles, backscenes etc. See *British Railway Modelling's Scenic Modelling* book for more information on these topics.

Is N or OO scale best for newcomers to the hobby?

Both are very good starting points. Each scale is supported by a huge range of manufacturers. Around two thirds of modellers of those working in these two scales work in OO (and HO scales overseas).

The answer will depend very much on personal preference:
- If you want a relatively small layout, N scale may be best
- If you want a railway to run 'in the landscape', N scale might be best if the space you have available for a model railway is limited
- If your layout is a project with a young person, OO scale might be best – its locomotives are easier to handle
- If you enjoy fine detailing locomotives and scenes, then OO might be the most suitable. The possibilities for these in N scale are a little more limited.
- Some modellers find as they get older the larger scales are more suitable for their eyesight.

Holcombe Valley. How to build this simple scene was described on pages 30 to 32 of *Scenic Modelling* published by *BRM* in February 2008.

A tiny layout based on the BR Blue years.

The baseboard for this layout measured just 1.5 metres x 0.4 metres. Because of its compact dimensions, the layout was easy to move from its storage position against a wall, positioned on top of my desk and provide a quick way of running trains.

The baseboard was made from a 'Sundeala' top with planed timber supporting frame. To avoid fouling the printer next to my desk, I installed short legs of 15cm fixed to the underside of the baseboard. These legs meant that the layout sat above the printer.

The track plan was simplicity itself. It was just a single through line passing a basic halt with a yard of two short sidings. The track design is based on the Inglenook shunting formation, but provided scope for future growth by adding other baseboards either side of this board. In that way the siding next to the 'main line' could be extended to form a run-round loop. Indeed, both sidings could be extended in the same way.

RocoLine HO track was used because it is easy to lay and is ready ballasted. The rail is Code 83, so it looks good

AIMS OF THE LAYOUT
- To make a layout that was easy to move and set up
- To make a layout that could be extended
- To represent a secondary line in BR blue days

once it is weathered. Because the track stands high (the point motors can be fixed underneath the ballast), it was necessary to build up the adjacent landscape to disguise some of the height of the ballast on what was supposed to be a secondary branch line. I used mounting card for this purpose. The weathering of the rails and ballast was done with brush painted acrylic paints.

Control was just two wires into the track from a Gaugemaster Combi unit. What simplicity! But the result was that I could be running trains smoothly and slowly within five minutes of the removal of the layout from its storage position and installed on top of the desk.

Scenery and the details

The scenery formers were 3mm cardboard filled with crumpled newspaper and covered with two layers of Mod Roc plaster impregnated cloth. This was painted with acrylics when dry (the next day) and then covered with Silflor 'magic carpet' spread over PVA adhesive. I acquired a sheet of the short grass spring (710-21) from International Models after reading about the product in the model press. This was the first time that I used this but the result was pleasing. The 'grass' is not flat and the wide variety of the products in the range – short, long, pasture, and pasture with weeds in four seasons - deserve attention.

The additional undergrowth was mainly Woodland Scenics products – Fine Leaf Foliage and Clump Foliage. The trees were a mixture from various manufacturers - one K&M large deciduous specimen, two poplars from Heki, several conifers from Architrees of Chicago and a couple of other large deciduous trees from Model Masters.

LAYOUT PROFILE
Size: 1.5 m x 0.4 m (5'0" x 1"4")
Country: UK
Location: West Country
Track: RocoLine ready ballasted
Control: Gaugemaster Combi
Scenics: Silflor and Woodland Scenics
Trees: Heki, Architrees, K&M and others
Buildings: Ratio and Wills

This layout was built to stand on short legs on the author's writing desk. The legs raised the layout over the printer to the right-hand side of the picture.

There were just two buildings on the layout - a small signal cabin and a small station building from the Wills and Ratio ranges. Both were brush painted with acrylics and detailed. The platform was made from 3mm cardboard, painted with acrylics and finished with Ratio fencing and a variety of waiting passengers.

The shape of the pond was made from Mod Roc plaster impregnated cloth and the floor of the pond was painted with a variety of acrylics. Once the paint was dry two thin layers of the

Platform end at Torcombe/ The poplar trees are by Heki, the fence by Ratio as is the signal box. The gas lamp is an old one by Merit - now Model Scene.

Woodland Scenics Realistic Water were poured in and then left for 24 hours to dry. A rather strange looking swan was resident on the water.

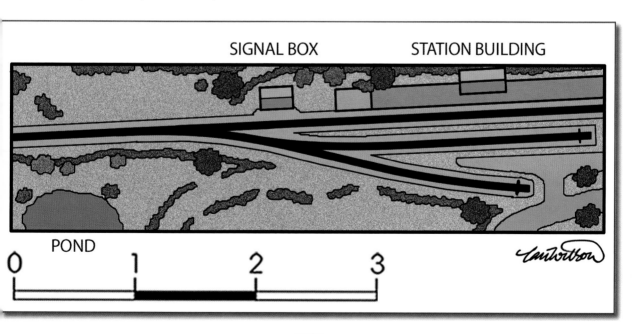

SIGNAL BOX   STATION BUILDING

POND

0   1   2   3

Weathered Hornby Class 22 locomotive shunts a newspaper van on a sunny summer day.

A Hornby Class 25 locomotive shunts in the yard.

A converted Lima DMU became this Class 121 single car unit. Hornby have now reintroduced this model with better livery detail and running abilities.

A busy day at Torcombe! Passengers climb aboard the Class 121 unit whilst the Class 25 shunts in the yard.

SETTING THE SCENE

Locomotive, Scots Pine and backscene.

A small West Highland locomotive stabling point modelled to demonstrate how details define an area.

When we build layouts we usually want to reproduce how an area looks in reality. Whether it be a Western Region branch line in Somerset or a Scottish single track line, each area has maybe up to a dozen defining features special to it.

So, for example, a Scottish line might have:

- A single-track line
- Scots Pine trees
- Heather
- Pink ballast
- Scottish Region station name boards

- A Class 37/4 locomotive with three Mk.1 carriages (in the 1990s)
- A few deer and walkers
- A small rusting corrugated permanent way hut painted apple green
- Distant hills

By contrast a Western Region branch line summer scene of 1957 might feature:

- Again a single-track line
- Milk churns on station platforms
- A busy goods yard
- Western Region station name boards
- A Pannier tank with a couple of

chocolate and cream carriages
- A lot of holidaymakers waiting on station platforms
- Rolling hills
- Verdant hedgerows and fields
- A few motor vehicles of the 1950s

It is these defining details that will add to the realism of any layout.

For the purpose of this chapter, we have built a small diorama of a tiny corner of a West Highland Line locomotive stabling point. We shall endeavour to demonstrate how we have used the appropriate details to try to define the location and the approximate date of the scene.

Making West Fort Yard

The size of the diorama was determined by the size of an off-cut piece of plywood that I had to hand – this was 56 cms x 20 cms. To ensure that the plywood would remain in shape, I fixed a light timber frame to it using PVA and panel pins.

The small size of the diorama limited the amount of trackwork and scenery that could be accommodated. So rather than attempting to put any pointwork on the baseboard, I restricted the trackwork to just two pieces of straight track. The shorter section could be used as a storage line for a fuel oil tanker or for storing a Class 08 or Class 20 locomotive. The longer line could be used to display a Class 37/4 locomotive.

Fixing the track down was very easy. I just marked around the track with a pencil and brushed on a generous amount of PVA in the place that the track was to be positioned - I used a 1" decorating brush for this. I then pushed the track down centrally into the adhesive and sprinkled on some RIKO fine cork ballast that I have had in stock for more than 20 years. I used cork rather than the more usual fine granite because, to my eye, it gave the impression of the West Highland salmon pink ballast fairly well. Once the PVA had dried – a few hours later – I shook off the surplus ballast and tipped it back into its storage jar to re-use it at some later date.

In between the rails, I dabbed a few spots of PVA and pushed home several Silflor Grass Tufts. These gave the appearance of a little-used industrial siding.

To add a little variety to the appearance of the yard, I used one Peco rail-built buffer stop and another Peco product, a sleeper-built buffer stop, for the other line. Both were painted with matt acrylics. A few weeds were planted around the base of these using a dab or

DIORAMA PROFILE

Size:	0.56 m x 0.20 m (1'10" x 8")
Country:	UK
Location:	A small diesel stabling point on the West Highland line in the 1990s
Track:	Peco flexible
Ballast:	Riko fine cork
Control:	none
Scenics:	Heki, Noch, Scenic Express, Treemendus and Woodland Scenics
Trees:	4D Model Shop

two of PVA and some Heki foliage mat.

To the rear of the diorama I wanted a low bank bordering the site of the diesel stabling point. The reason for this bank was:
- It would provide somewhere to plant some excellent Scots Pine trees that I

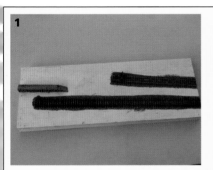

1. The diorama with track laid and low wall in place.

2. Building up the embankment.

3. Plaster cloth laid on the embankment.

4. Painted plaster cloth with rail-built buffer stop.

5. Sleeper-built buffer stop.

6. Wills cobblestone sheet laid alongside the track.

7

7. Treemendus tall grass planted at the rear of the diorama.

8

8. Foliage and tall grass.

9

9. A clump of heather on the embankment.

10

10. Two Scots Pines by 4D Model Shop showing planting pins.

11

JL INNOVATIVE DESIGN

CUSTOM OIL BARRELS
(Pre-painted & labeled)

HO SCALE

#569 Conoco Barrels

11. Detailed oil drums by US Manufacturer JL Innovative Design.

12

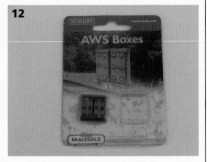

HORNBY

AWS Boxes

SKALEDALE

12. AWS box by Hornby Skaledale.

13

TREEMENDUS
Quality handmade scale model trees and scenic modelling materials

13. Fake teddy bear fur by Treemendus for tall grass and cornfields.

14

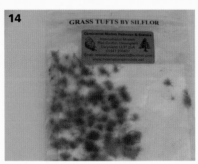

GRASS TUFTS BY SILFLOR

14. Grass Tufts by Silflor for weeds and other taller grasses.

15

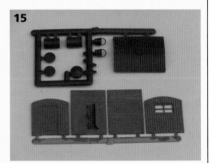

15. Wills platelayers hut kit painted to resemble a West Highland hut.

16

16. Pallet and load by Ten Commandments.

17

17. The completed scene.

18

ESSO

18. Esso fuel tanker by Bachmann/Modelzone.

had obtained from the 4D Model Shop. It was important that these trees would form part of the scene, because they would provide the necessary Scottish flavour.

- Somewhere to plant a little heather to add further to the Scottish flavour of the scene
- It would provide an intermediate visual link between the diesel depot and the distant hills.

To build the bank, I used mounting card to form the rear and side wall of the bank. This was fixed to the plywood baseboard with PVA and once this had dried, the shape of the bank was formed from packing paper from a parcel that had arrived a couple of days before. The packing paper was held in place temporarily with a few of pieces of sellotape. Two layers of wet plaster cloth by Woodland Scenics was laid on top of the packing material and then left to dry. When the plaster cloth was dry it was painted using brown acrylic paint. This dark colour was used to stop the white of

the plaster showing through when the scenic materials were added at the next stage.

The landscaping on the bank was a mixture of Noch static grasses and Scenic Express 'Flock and Turf'. Both used PVA to fix them to the bank. I chose subdued greens and light browns to represent the tints of autumn. Some clumps of heather were added to the banks using PVA. These were small sections of a 4D Model Shop heather texture mat.

In the right-hand rear corner of the diorama, I wanted some tall grass to give the impression of a weed-strewn area. To make these weeds I used Treemendus fake teddy bear fur. A piece of it was cut to fill the area and fixed to the baseboard, using PVA brushed onto the underside of the fur. The fur stands over 2 cms tall, so I roughly trimmed the top with scissors to leave a rather ragged effect. Once the fur was firmly fixed to the base, I used acrylic paint applied with a pair of rubber gloves in a motion that works through the fur from each angle.

The general area around the sidings was intended to look run-down and industrial with the grassy bank, foliage, heather, backscene and trees offering the only glimpses of Scottish scenery. I used a section of Noch hardfoam wall at the front of the bank to represent the location of an earlier goods platform, when the railways were more important to the Scottish Highlands. I found that the hardfoam rock walling was easy to cut with a sharp craft knife. It comes in a variety of colours.

Alongside the main siding, a section of Wills cobblestones sheet was stuck down with PVA. This was to introduce a different element of surface texture into the yard. It was painted with various acrylic paints to represent an oily surface.

The earth around the yard was painted with PVA and then Treemendus earth colour (very fine real earth) was sprinkled over it by hand.

To detail the scene, I used a variety of

19. Two Scots Pines by 4D Model Shop planted on the embankment.

20. AWS box by Hornby Skaledale in situ on the diorama.

21. Oil drums and palleted load by Wills, JL Innovative Design and Life Like Scene Master.

22. ViTrains 37/4 locomotive.

23. Scenic Express scatter materials.

24. Class 37/4 locomotive *Mary Queen of Scots*

	Manufacturer	Suppliers
SCENICS		
Plaster cloth	Woodland Scenics	www.bachmann.co.uk for dealers
Scatter materials	Scenic Express	www.modeljunction.info
Static grass	Noch	www.gaugemaster.com
Weeds in track	Silflor	www.internationalmodels.net
Tall grass	Treemendus	www.treemendusmodels.co.uk
Foliage	Heki	www.javis.co.uk
Scots Pines	4 D ModelShop	www.modelshop.co.uk
Heather	4 D ModelShop	www.modelshop.co.uk
YARD		
Cobblestones	Wills	www.peco-uk.com for list of dealers
Stone wall	Noch	www.gaugemaster.com
Ballast	Riko fine cork	Similar from www.gaugemaster.com
Buffer stops	Peco	www.peco-uk.com for list of dealers
Earth	Treemendus	www.treemendusmodels.co.uk
DETAILS		
AWS boxes	Hornby	www.hornby.com for list of dealers
Figures	Preiser	www.gaugemaster.com
Pallets & sacks	Ten Commandments	www.cast-in-stone.co.uk
Pallets & boxes	Life Like	www.modeljunction.info
Named oil drums	JL Innovations	www.modeljunction.info
Plain oil drums	Wills	www.peco-uk.com for list of dealers

products from different manufacturers:

- An AWS box from the Hornby Skaledale range
- Oil drums by JL Innovative Design (a US product sold in the UK by Model Junction) and Wills
- A few depot figures by Preiser
- Some pallets and loads by Ten Commandments and the Scene Master range by Life Like

The backscene was painted by brush using a mixture of acrylic paints. For the photographs I located it a few inches behind the baseboard to give a little more distant effect.

The diorama now stands on top of my desk and provides somewhere to stand my latest locomotive.

Preserved lines offer a great way to get inspiration for your next layout.

Shunter 08 168 stands in the main platform at Shackerstone waiting for customers to take cab rides in the yard.

The main station building is an impressive affair. The cafe is good too!

Shenton Station
Bosworth Battlefield

This line is located near to the famous Bosworth site. An ideal excuse for a family day out!

Getting the steam up!

Preserved lines are not only home to small locomotives. Here 1306 works a special train in March 2008.

THE MAYFLOWER

No 1306

The beautifully rebuilt station at the Shenton terminus of the line.

VALUE FOR MONEY MODELLING

Whilst some of us may like the idea of building a model railway, the cost of some of the latest products such as locomotives may seem to be rather daunting. This may apply to a young person living on pocket money or someone with large family commitments. Does that mean that these folk will not be able to have a model railway of their own? Certainly not. We'll list a few possible solutions.

Do not ignore the second-hand market. Many models that have been acquired as collectors' items are in mint and boxed condition. These usually represent good value for money if you choose to buy those products with long product runs. Second-hand models may be found on eBay, in magazine adverts, at second-hand dealers, at Toy and Collectors Fairs and from personal contact made at model railway shows or clubs.

If one's budget is limited to purchasing locomotives and rolling stock, why not join your local model railway club? You'll be able to assist on their layout building projects and hopefully you will be given running rights over some of their layouts.

A small layout may be all that one's pocket will accommodate but, in my experience, it will be more satisfying to own and operate if it is stocked with a few good quality locomotives rather than an extensive fleet of mediocre models. There is nothing more vexing that having five locomotives of which only two run really well and the others stutter on the points and are generally poor runners.

Consider part exchanging your current equipment for something that takes your fancy at a different stage in your modelling career. There are numerous companies and dealers advertising to acquire second-hand equipment and offering part exchange.

Some companies retail train sets (sometimes known as start sets), in both OO and N scale, that offer excellent value for money. These sets usually include a locomotive, some rolling stock, at least a circle of track and a controller/transformer. These companies also usually retail track packs that can be used to expand upon the start set in stages.

European manufacturers such as Bemo (narrow gauge), Fleischmann, Roco and Trix retail start sets. UK

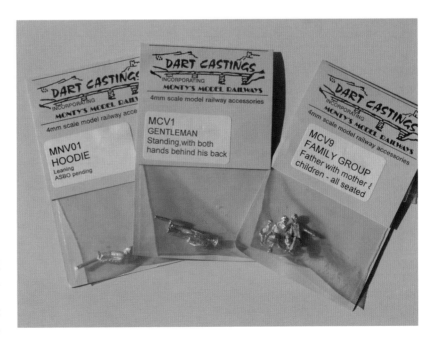

If you are considering making the step to DCC, look at the train set packs that include a DCC system. Sometimes the price of these sets is less than the control system itself.

There are a few additional cost-cutting tips that may be used:

- Buy unpainted people rather than the finished products
- Scratch-build your own catenary buildings, trees
- Buy trees in bulk and detail them yourself if necessary
- Go green - use parcel packing (that would otherwise be thrown away) as the basis for your hillsides and embankments
- Purchase PVA adhesive in bulk if you intend to make a lot of scenery
- Buy flexible track in bulk

In summary, search the magazine advertisements, look on dealer's shelves, buy sets rather than individual parts, visit second-hand dealers and scan the internet for bargains!

Lastly, learn patience. Though we may want all our favourite locomotives immediately, it's more satisfying to build up a collection slowly. After all if you have everything today, what have you left to look forward to?

modellers should not ignore these sets, because some of the track systems are good and coupled with their good control systems are worth buying, even if you do not wish to use the European locomotive and rolling stock.

Major manufacturers such as Bachmann and Hornby now have 'entry-level' locomotives that have most of the positive qualities of their dearer brothers, except the price and a few details. The Bachmann Junior range and Hornby's Railroad range are important recent innovations in the hobby.

Some of the larger model railway shows and Toy Fairs feature 'special show offers' on sets and model railway equipment, that make the payment of the entrance ticket worthwhile.

There are some European and US locomotive models that have good running qualities, remarkably low prices and may be repainted and detailed to represent industrial shunting locos working in private sidings on UK layouts.

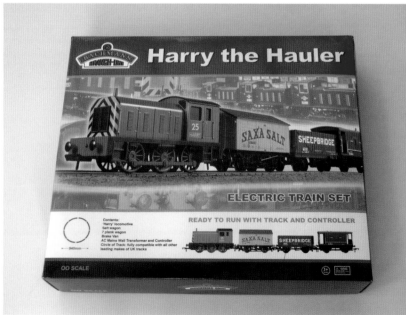

Being Kent, the Class 92s can be seen passing through Ashdown *en route* from the Channel Tunnel.

A basic trainset oval with a loop.

The baseboard for this layout used planed 44mm x 19mm timber for the frame, nailed together using wire nails. Holes were drilled into the timber (before nailing) to prevent the wood splitting on assembly. A sheet of 9mm medium density fibreboard (MDF) was used for the baseboard top. It was fixed to the framework using a little PVA woodworking glue and 50mm wire nails. Additional holes were drilled in the underframe pieces before assembly,

AIMS OF THE LAYOUT
- To demonstrate what can be achieved with a train set
- To use readily available products
- To represent a small passing station in Kent

to enable wires to pass between the cross-members.

Whilst a baseboard measuring 137mm x 94mm might sound small on paper, when you begin to move it

around the house it begins to take on large proportions! Moving a layout of this size upstairs or downstairs is usually a two-man job, even for such a compact layout such as this.

Because this was intended to demonstrate what can be done with a trainset we used just the track pieces supplied in a Fleischmann Start Set. The track was Fleischmann HO Profi-Track which is ready ballasted. Their range of track parts is extensive, including an electric turntable, manual or electric

BR Blue and preserved steam seen together.

LAYOUT PROFILE
Size: 1.37m x 0.94m (4'6" x 3'1")
Country: UK
Location: Kent
Track: Fleischmann Profi ready ballasted (from the Start Set)
Control: Fleischmann controller (from the Start Set)
Scenics: Woodland Scenics foliage, hedging and scatter material
Trees: Sea Foam
Buildings: Airfix (now Dapol), Peco, Ratio, Wills and a *BRM* free gift

points, slot-in board point motors, etc. The sectional track used for this layout took less than five minutes to lay! The track was lightly nailed to the board at about 40 cm intervals.

The track was placed off-centre to get away from the 'train set oval on baseboard' look. This is a useful technique to disguise a symmetrical track plan. The loop at the front formed a small local passing station with a level crossing to the rear.

Building the scenery used long standing simple methods – mounting card for the landscape formers, crumpled up newspaper pushed between the formers and then covered in Mod-Roc plaster impregnated cloth. Once the cloth was dry, it was painted with acrylics to stop the white Mod-Roc showing through if the scatter material wears a little thin! A variety of scatter material colours and shades were mixed, with the final coat containing some finely chopped foam pieces for added effect.

The platforms were made from 3mn mounting card, with Superquick bric paper covered walls. The top surface o the platforms was two layers of ver fine black scatter material sprinkle over PVA.

The five buildings on the layout wer from a variety of manufacturers. Th thatch applied to the roof of the olc Airfix plastic kit cottage was plumber': hemp. My wife spent many hour: cutting the hemp to size and then gluing it to the card roof in stages. Not a tasl to be hurried! Use plastic sheets of tiles if you are in a rush to finish the layout The country house was a kit built from Wills parts and the permanent way hu' was a free card kit given away in *Britis* *Railway Modelling* magazine. The Peco station building was painted using acrylics. The stonework was given a little dry brushing to highlight the cornerstones and door/window inserts. The SR concrete platelayers hut was one of the Ratio plastic kits – it was very simple to build and is a good beginners kit.

Hedging was foam clusters from Woodland Scenics. The tunnel used Merit tunnel mouths that were painted and weathered. The people dotted around the station area are ready painted figures by Merit plus a few hand-painted ones from Dapol.

STATION

TUNNEL

LEVEL CROSSING

0   1   2   3

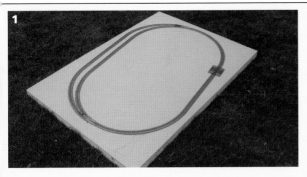

1. The baseboard was made from a sheet of 9mm MDF glued and nailed to a frame of 44 mm x 19 mm planed timber. The Fleischmann track has been lightly pinned to the board – note that it was laid at an angle to the sides of the board.

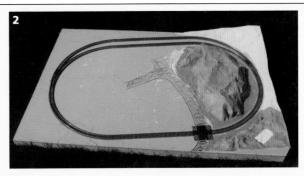

2. The next stage was to begin to build up the scenery. Card formers made from mounting card were fiied around the right-hand side of the baseboard to form the sides of the cuttings and banks. These were then filled with crumpled up newspaper and covered with plaster impregnated cloth. Once the plaster was dry, the surface was painted with green acrylics.

3. The platforms were made from mounting card, with the walls covered in Superquick brick paper. The buildings were positioned on the layout and roads marked on the baseboard.

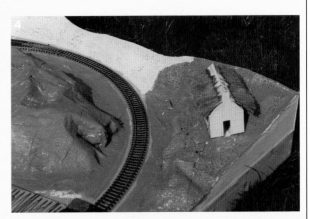

4. An Airfix (now Dapol) thatched cottage under construction using plumber's hemp to represent the thatch. This is at an early stage of the scenery showing the card formers and partially painted plaster cloth.

5. Various stages of the scenery construction with unpainted plaster cloth, painted cloth, first coating of scatter materials and final detailing of foliage, vegetation, etc.

6. House built from Wills plastic sheets. The fitting of curtains and drainpipes are important in adding realism. The white brickwork was dry-brushed with a little grey acrylic paint to give the effect of relief and weathered brickwork.

7. Another Lima DMU, this time a Class 156 set in Regional Railways colours.

8. Single car Class DMU in BR Blue (Lima model modified from a two car set) calls at Ashdown station. The station buildings are a kit by Peco, repainted and detailed.

9. The station plays host to two steam locomotives of the local preservation society for the day. Depicted is a Dapol 'Terrier' 0-6-0 in Southern livery and a Bachmann J72 in BR colours.

10. A local preservation society special passenger service with Dapol 'Terrier' 0-6-0 in Southern livery heading a Hornby corridor coach.

A diorama of a tiny German wayside halt.

Dioramas can be a useful way to experiment with new modelling techniques, new products and even to explore countries that we are not familiar with. Dioramas can be built in a matter of days and may be used to form the basis of a later layout.

The diorama illustrated here was based around a Fides HO scale kit of Reinstetten station. Whilst Reinstetten is located in southern Germany in Bavaria this station halt is not a faithful copy of the prototype.

The diorama was mainly built from 'bits and pieces' that I happened to have to hand from earlier projects. The baseboard measured 1m x 25cm and

> ## AIMS OF THE LAYOUT
> - To demonstrate what can be achieved on a one metre off-cut baseboard
> - To use a timber built building kit
> - To represent a small passing station in Germany

was just a plywood off-cut that I found in our garage. The track was mainly Peco, using Riko fine cork for ballast.

The platform was made from 3mm cardboard, with fine black scenic scatter material representing the tarmac top surface. A Merit gas lamp was used on

the platform. The passengers were by Preiser.

A variety of scatter materials were used for the flat landscaping, including Woodland Scenics and Heki. The trees are Heki Scots Pines built from one of their tree packs. Road vehicles are a mixture of Herpa and Wiking models.

The station building kit, which unusually features timber parts, rather than the more familiar plastic components, costs around £25. It has pre-cut wood pieces, plastic window frames, drainpipes and various detailing parts. There is a useful exploded diagram to assist with construction. The walls were brush painted with

LAYOUT PROFILE
Size: 1m x 0.25m (3'4" x 10")
Country: Germany
Location: No definite location
Track: Peco
Control: Hammant & Morgan Clipper
Scenics: Heki and Woodland Scenics
Trees: Heki
Buildings: Fides

Fleischmann DB Class 212 locomotive passes Reinstetten.

acrylics and for the construction of the kit I used PVA woodworking adhesive. I decided to build the model with the lean-to structure as a separate small goods shed, rather than form part of the main station building. I found this kit fun and easy to build. Fides kits are available from Great Little Trains (www.greatlittletrains.com).

The advantages of joining a model railway club

Clubs are a fine place to mix with fellow enthusiasts. The advantages can be summarised as follows:

- Clubs generally have several layouts under construction in various scales. You'll be able to assist with building these.
- You'll have the chance to run your own locomotives and rolling stock on a lot larger layout than would be possible at home.
- Do not be put off because you are new to the hobby. There will always be folks willing to show you the best way to do most modelling tasks.
- The opportunity to assist on the layouts at model railway exhibitions.
- Some clubs have 'junior' modellers' sections. What a great way for young people to keep out of trouble!

The locomotives in the pictures are a mixture of German Railways (DB) Class 120 and 212. They were manufactured by Fleischmann and Piko. The wagons are from the ranges of Jouef, Fleischmann and Lima.

Although the diorama was built utilising German rolling stock and buildings, the concept could be equally applied to any European country. Replace the Scots Pine trees with bulb fields and erect Dutch buildings for a rural Netherlands scene!

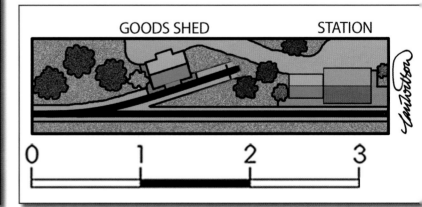

DETAILING A DIESEL LOCOMOTIVE

Many of today's ready-to-run diesel, electric and steam locomotives in OO, HO, TT and N scale arrive with a small plastic bag containing detailing parts to be fitted by the purchaser. Some purchasers fit these parts to their loco but others do not.

Whilst the locomotives do look better with the parts attached, there are various reasons why purchasers decide not to fit them. These include:
• If the purchaser is a collector of locomotive models he may consider that his locomotive is no longer in 'mint and boxed' condition following the fitment of the parts.
• Some of the parts are rather fiddly to

fit. The more nimble one's fingers, the better for this task.
• Some prefer to operate their locomotives with tension lock couplings on both ends of a model, but the fitment of these couplings might not be possible if the details are fitted.

Before starting work on detailing the locomotive, it is worth referring to the various prototype motive power books that are available. These include *Cades Locomotive Guide* that provides information about all British Outline models (for more information see www. cadeslocomotiveguide.co.uk). These books contain illustrations showing

where to fix the various pipes, nameplates, air horns, buffer beam details, etc.

Manufacturers supply a pictorial guide showing where the parts are to be inserted on the model. Sometimes they recommend that parts be glued to the model, sometimes they do not comment. Personally I like to dab a tiny drop of contact adhesive on each part where it is joins the locomotive. In that way I am pretty sure they will not fall off during transit.

The minimum tools that are needed for loco detailing projects are: contact adhesive, superglue, a small file, a sharp craft knife, a small pair of tweezers and a small paintbrush. Some acrylic paints may be needed to touch-up the final

Space limitations might tie one's hands in this decision, but in general terms having a continuous run is generally a good move:

- It's good to be able to run new purchases
- New locomotives usually need a period of 'running in' in both directions before they are slow running and smooth in operation.
- Most of us like to see trains in action and even if one's main interest is building a layout running trains is fun.
- Visitors who might have heard about our hobby expect to see some trains in motion!

product – these would include yellow, red, black and weathering colours.

Different manufacturers supply less or more detailing parts. For example, a Bachmann OO scale Class 57 locomotive comes with the following additional parts to be fitted - two nameplates, two roof aerials and six pipes for each cab end.

In contrast a ViTrains Class 37/4 locomotive comes complete with six plastic sprues in black and yellow plus six other parts. In total there over 65 additional parts supplied. Not all could be fitted to the one locomotive – some of the parts are supplied in case you mislay a part.

Diesel models have various small holes in the buffer beam, cab front, cab roof and bogie to push the parts into. I find that some of these holes are a little on the tight side and occasionally a little expanding of the hole is necessary with a very small diameter file.

When ready to position the detail part on the locomotive, I brush a little contact adhesive onto the plug on the pipe and then push them into the relevant hole using finger power. Some might find a pair of tweezers assists this process.

When the pipes are fixed firmly to the locomotive – the adhesive usually dries in well under an hour – the connections on the pipes can be highlighted using yellow or orange acrylic paint. Look at photos of the real thing to see which pipes are painted which colour.

Adding the roof-mounted air horns and hood-mounted aerials is simply done by putting a little contact adhesive into the hole with a very fine paintbrush and then pushing home the aerials (be careful that they are vertical) and horns.

Where manufacturers supply nameplates, they sometimes usefully print a location guide on the side of the locomotive. These guides make the fitting of nameplates a lot easier. It is necessary to carefully cut the nameplates from the metal strip and then fix the plate to the locomotive side with a small amount of superglue.

This detailing work on one end of a diesel locomotive usually takes a minimum of an hour. The purchaser can choose whether he wants to fit the parts on both ends or just one.

I think that most modellers would agree that a detailed locomotive looks a lot more realistic than the version straight from the box. And most have found that detailing a locomotive certainly gives a lot of satisfaction to the person who has done the work.

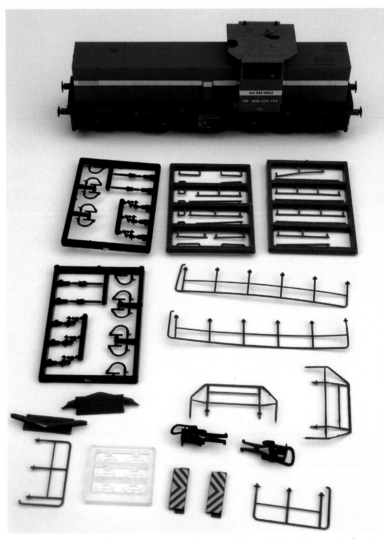

Liliput Swiss Bo-Bo diesel locomotive in HO scale comes with a profusion of parts to be fitted.

N scale is ideal for short trains – this one measure just 16 cms! A 3F Fowler tank leaves with one mineral wagon and brake van.

A basic continuous run line in N scale.

This demonstration layout is intended to depict a single line in the country with a two siding goods yard. There are just a couple of buildings, a few fields, some trees, a winding country lane and a scenic ridge running across the layout.

The layout would be suitable for someone either making his first model railway in any scale, or indeed his first excursion into N scale. It could accommodate a couple of locomotives and a few wagons. It is basically just a

AIMS OF THE LAYOUT
- To build an N gauge continuous layout using a track starter kit and ready-to-go materials from a variety of manufacturers
- To build a layout on one small baseboard that can be easily stored and set up ready to operate within a few minutes
- To build a basic layout within 10 hours

very short step on from a trainset.

Everything used on this layout is 'ready-to-run'. The track used is the track from the Peco Setrack starter kit plus two short straights used in the goods yard. The track runs on top of Gaugemaster ballast roll.

The buildings are Hornby Lyddle End and the trees are from The Model Tree Shop. The scenic ridge running across the layout with the railway line cutting through was made from a Woodland Scenics Landform - we cut this into two pieces (with scissors) to fit the layout.

The layout can be stored under a bed, on top of a freestanding wardrobe, on brackets in a garage or just simply standing up against a wall. Apart from the occasional need to clean the track the layout could be retrieved from its storage position and placed on the floor, a desk, a table or even a kitchen top, plugged into the mains and away you go. If this type of layout is used on a table or any other surface, use a table protector to ensure the domestic

LAYOUT PROFILE
Size: 1 m x 0.60 m (3'4" x 2'0")
Country: UK
Location: A single track secondary line somewhere in Derbyshire
Track: Peco Setrack starter kit plus two Peco short straights
Control: Gaugemaster Combi
Scenics: Faller, Noch, Treemendus and Woodland Scenics
Trees: The Model Tree Shop
Buildings: Hornby Lyddle End

authorities are comfortable with model railways being used in the 'household areas'!

The layout did indeed take less than 10 hours to make. Breaking this down, it took one hour to build the baseboard, two hours to lay the track and fit the ballast strip, one hour to make the scenic ridge and another four hours to scenic the layout, make the roads, plant the hedges and trees and fix the accessories such as the telegraph poles and buildings.

The entire finished layout waiting for a coat of finishing paint around its timber frame edge.

Here we see the whole layout at track on baseboard stage. The track on this layout is the track from the Peco N scale Starter Set plus the addition of two short straights to extend the sidings.

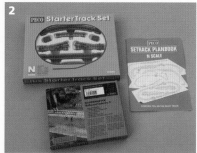

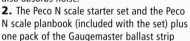

1. Close up of the track showing the sectional pieces in Gaugemaster ballast strip (stock number GM 201). This ballast is sold in five metre rolls. For points the strip needs to be cut centrally and then another 'V' section of ballast inlay inserted. On the plain track the sleepers just push home into the slots on the ballast strip. The result is a nicely raised strip of ballast with real granite stone chippings bonded onto the shoulders that also absorbs noise.

2. The Peco N scale starter set and the Peco N scale planbook (included with the set) plus one pack of the Gaugemaster ballast strip (this product is made for Gaugemaster by Noch).

3. Once the track was laid, the baseboard was painted with acrylics using a wide flat brush – green where there will be grass and foliage, grey where there will be roads, a goods yard and soil.

4. To make a scenic ridge running across the right-hand side of the layout I used a Woodland Scenics Ready Landform. These pieces are sold as tunnels and curved ridges. The base material is blown plastic but then they are covered with scatter materials and some clump foliage. The rock faces are painted.

5. This shows that the Woodland Scenics Ready Landform is hollow – this was one of the large Curved Ridges. I cut it with scissors to form two sections – one on either side of the track.

6. The 'hole' in the cut Ready Landform has been filled with Woodland Scenics plaster cloth. I used two layers for good rigidity.

7. The plaster cloth was painted black with Reeves ready mixed poster colour.

8. Woodland Scenics Plaster Cloth, Hobbycraft PVA and Reeves ready mixed poster paint purchased from a discount bookstore.

9. The mid way stage of the layout. The road has been laid (mounting card), the bare baseboard has been painted with acrylic and posters paints, the ridge and cutting have been fixed in place.

10. The first application of fine scatter material as applied to one corner of the layout. Anita Décor fine foam was sprinkled on top of brushed on PVA.

11. To the left is a section of the moulded Gaugemaster ballast strip. To the right is a Javis roll of hedging.

12. Noch N scale figures and Ratio telegraph poles.

13. The range of Hornby's Lyddle End building and scenic accessories is expanding each year. The resin buildings come ready-painted and finished and can be positioned on the layout immediately. One can weather the buildings a little if desired using dry-brushing techniques.

15. The hedges on the layout were a Javis product fixed to the baseboard with PVA. Then PVA was brushed across the hedge and fine quality light green scenic scatter sprinkled on to add more texture. The apple tree is by The Model Tree Shop – the glossy apples look larger in the photograph than in real life!

14. On the layout we used the Hornby Love Lane Cottage as the main building. Here it stands in front of the Woodland Scenics Ready Landform ridge.

16. Once the open end of the Woodland Scenics Ready Landform was fully sceniced it blended well with the other part.

17. Close up of Love Lane Cottage.

18. N gauge wagons do not have to be devoid of detail – this Graham Farish private owner wagon has excellent print detail.

19. 20 ton LMS brake van.

20. BR liveried Fowler 4F locomotive by Graham Farish (as are all of the locomotives depicted).

21. A BR 4MT 2-6-4 tank locomotive simmers in the yard.

22. Ratio telegraph pole and tree from The Model Tree Shop.

23. Shunting taking place in the yard.

24. A 'Crab' 2-6-0 moves a train of open wagons towards Derby.

25. A simple scene 'out in the country' with telegraph pole, weathered track and a train spotter sitting in the 1978 Ford Fairmont car by Atlas.

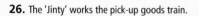

26. The 'Jinty' works the pick-up goods train.

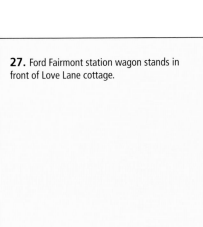

27. Ford Fairmont station wagon stands in front of Love Lane cottage.

28. The difference a little weathering makes to the rails and sleepers.

29. A silghtly different layout - with no goods yard. This is what a basic oval of track would look like.

MAKING A RAIL BRIDGE

This is the Whimple Bridge that was described and illustrated in the *BRM Scenic Modelling book*. The same West Highland liveried Class 37/4 locomotive gets around! The bridge is one of the excellent resin castings by Hornby Skaledale.

Layouts that feature scenery which is only built up from the baseboard lack the depth that we see in real life. Railway lines often run on the top of embankments, across roads or rivers and along viaducts in cities. With the recent arrival of a wide range of bridges from Kibri, Hornby and other companies, the task of making bridges has become easier.

On one layout, I used weathered RocoLine track with its built-in ballast, in conjunction with a Roco straight bridge that fitted the track geometry. The bridge was Roco 05083A (Kastenbrucke), which was 23 cms long.

I located the bridge at an angle to the baseboard edge and raised the track on timber formers on the front of the baseboard that were 8 cms lower than the rear of the baseboard.

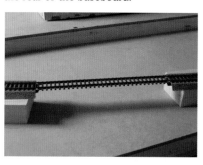

Location of the bridge. Adjacent track raised up to the level of the bridge.

The Roco bridge was very simple to build – it was just five main parts: the base, two girder sides and two timber walkways with fencing. Assembly took under five minutes. The kit pieces were

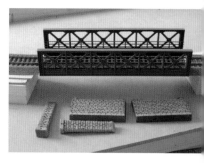

Bridge *in situ* with the cut pieces of Noch sandstone walling that will form the supporting walls.

Bridge positioned on top of the supporting walls, which match the adjacent retaining walls.

Aerial view of the bridge, showing the walkway and screw that gives a firm fix to the track.

Close up of one of the supporting walls. This was made from Noch hardfoam walling - it's easy to cut and light in weight.

Bridge in place with some of the scenic work complete. The water is still to be added.

moulded in light green plastic but I decided to paint the bridge pieces mid-grey with one-tenth rust colour. Acrylic paints were used, applied with a small brush. The walkway timbers were painted dark stain colour with the handrails light grey.

To provide the supporting walls for the bridge, I used sections of arcaded sandstone walling by Noch (58078). This wall is part of their hardfoam range of sandstone walling and tunnel portals in N, TT and HO scales. It was easy to cut with a sharp craft knife over a cutting board.

Once I had positioned the bridge in place on its supporting embankments, I built-up the surrounding land with cardboard formers and Woodland Scenics plaster cloth, wich was then covered in scatter materials.

Lone 37 402 *Oor Wullie* crosses the bridge.

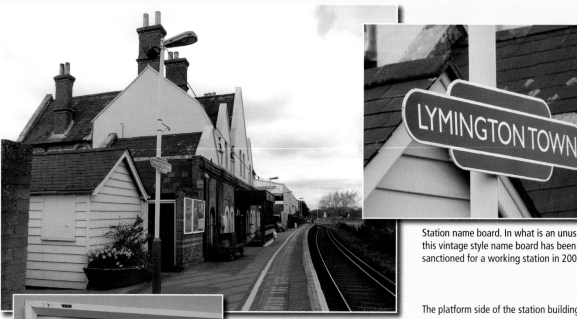

Station name board. In what is an unusual move, this vintage style name board has been sanctioned for a working station in 2008.

The platform side of the station buildings.

The sign on the station announcing that South West Trains are operating the line between Brockenhurst and Lymington as a Heritage Line.

Heritage trains on the Lymington Line

Two slam door trains, especially refurbished to their former glory and sporting original British Rail colours, now run between Lymington Town and Brockenhurst.

We have made extensive refurbishments, restoring these trains to their original condition whilst meeting modern day standards. A dedicated wheelchair space has been added plus some additional seating and cycle storage.

This Heritage Line is a partnership between rail companies, local businesses and the community. By purchasing these two trains outright we are able to make this line more cost effective, helping to safeguard its future and maintaining rail connections at Brockenhurst and ferry links to the Isle of Wight. Continual developments on this line will mean it will prosper for many years to come.

Your views are always welcome – please speak to any of my colleagues working on this line who I have asked to feed any comments back to me.

We hope you enjoy travelling with us and experiencing a part of railway history.

John Collins
Group Station Manager,
Heritage Line

HERITAGE LINE
A piece of railway tradition at the heart of the New Forest

SOUTH WEST TRAINS

Classic EMU in heritage green leaves Lymington Town for Lymington Pier.

A wooden wheelbarrow, a trolley and milk churns on a working passenger station in 2008!

One of the huts on the station is closed up and to the front of it is an old wooden boat filled with earth and flowers.

The road side of the station building.

A small passing station somewhere in the Alps.

I built this layout for the *Modelling European Railways* special *BRM* magazine back in 2002. I have to confess that I made more mistakes on it than any other layout I've built. Firstly, I did not weather the track – shiny track really does detract from the realism of a layout. Secondly, the idea of trying to model a location without a specific prototype was probably not a very good one. The layout turned out to look just that!

AIMS OF THE LAYOUT
- To build a first European layout
- To build a layout that combined both standard and narrow gauge track
- To represent a small branch line station that could be found within Germany, Austria or Switzerland

Thirdly, whilst rolling stock and locomotives are often mixed on European railways, I choose to mix locomotives and carriages that would in reality, never work together. The clash of liveries was just too striking. With confession time over, perhaps we can move onto some other aspects of the layout.

The layout was built to be portable for possible exhibition use. It could be carried in a medium sized car, eg:

LAYOUT PROFILE
Size: Three baseboards of 1.5 m x 0.4 m giving a total length of 4.5 m (14'9" x 1"4")
Country: Austria, Switzerland or Germany
Location: No definite location
Track: RocoLine ready-ballasted
Control: Gaugemaster Combi
Scenics: Woodland Scenics and Heki
Trees: Heki
Buildings: Fides, Kibri and a US kit

In addition to the standard gauge line there was a small siding used by the Swiss Rhätische Bahn at the front of the layout. The use of both standard and narrow gauge track provided a little validity to the suggestion that the layout was near to both Austria and Switzerland. The narrow gauge siding was installed with Sommerfeldt catenary whilst the standard gauge lines were diesel only.

Ready-ballasted RocoLine track was used on the standard gauge line. This was my first venture with this track. I found it to be easy to lay, reasonably realistic (though as I mentioned above, in hindsight, I should have weathered it), but best of all I found that the locomotives ran beautifully on it. I stored the layout on brackets in the garage and even when it had not been used for some months. a quick wipe over with a damp cloth and the trains were ready to go.

The electrics were very simple. The points were hand-operated and

Ford Focus, VW Golf or Vauxhall Astra. The three baseboards each measured 1.5 m x 0.4 m being made from 6 mm plywood on a frame of planed timber.

The project combined standard gauge HO track and narrow gauge HOm track using an 'end to end' format. The standard gauge track

layout was three hidden sidings on the left-hand baseboard, with a single line winding its way past a large chalet style farmhouse and a simple passing station on the central board. The right-hand board featured a goods siding to the front of the baseboard with two hidden sidings located behind a steep cliff.

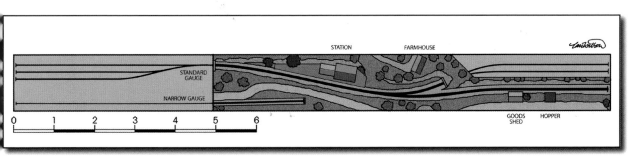

Above: The station building was made from a Fides kit which uses real wood parts.

Left: The goods shed used real pieces of metal for the roof cladding. The locomotive is by Klein Modellbahn.

A section of narrow gauge track was installed on the layout for variety. This picture depicts one of the well made HOm scale models by Bemo.

control was by a Gaugemaster Combi unit. I did have to make a few wire connections on the points to make them isolating.

I planted over 80 trees on the layout, most of which were by Heki. The rock faces were made from 'Tetrion', shaped with fingers and an old kitchen knife.

The station building is a Fides kit which, eagle eyed readers will notice, was carried over from my Reinstetten diorama. The large farmhouse was a Kibri plastic kit. The tall timber hopper building is a converted coaling stage built from a US kit some years ago. The majority of its parts are wood and it was painted using acrylics. It was intended to represent a lineside hopper on the layout.

The rolling stock was a mixture of Roco, Lima, Liliput, Fleischmann, Klein Modellbahn and Bemo.

UNDERGROUND ERNIE APPEALS TO CHILDREN!

Bachmann is producing an expanding range of model railway products based on the television series 'Underground Ernie'. The series is aimed at children aged between three and eight. It features the voices of Gary Lineker as Ernie and Janet Brown as Victoria. The underground trains include Bakerloo, Hammersmith and City, Jubilee and Victoria. In addition there are trains from other underground systems including Brooklyn (New York), Osaka, Paris, Moscow and Sydney.

The Underground Ernie 'Circle' range is being expanded by additional trains, track packs, buildings (including International Station, Industrial units, Mystery Mansion and Sports Stadium) and accessories. There are track packs that allow the track in the start sets to be extended as outlined on the track mat supplied in the set. For more information see www.bachmann.co.uk

Circle train calls at the station. The eyes on the train front move as the train makes its way around the track. Note the simple power connection.

Beneath the overall roof of International station.

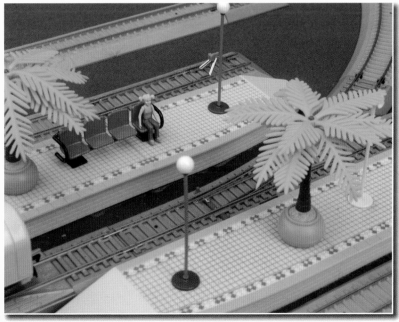

The accessories for these sets are attractive and colourful.

How to encourage children to become active railway modellers:

- Buy them a train set and help them (just enough!) to set it up and get some trains running.
- Buy a few accessories to increase the play value both of the initial purchase of the train set and at regular intervals thereafter to maintain their enthusiasm.
- Take children to model railway shows to show them trains running, but do not take them too often so that they tire of the hobby.
- Show them railway modelling magazines that are not too far beyond their ability to whet their appetite for the hobby.
- Encourage them to operate 'adult' model railways (under a degree of supervision!).
- Build them a model railway of their own. This can be compact and flat without scenery. It should include a continuous run track, even if it is just a circle, so they can see trains moving.
- Work with them to lay some track, to make buildings, to build some basic scenery and simply just design a trackplan. This will help them to widen their skills.
- Try to show children that railway modelling is a more constructive and satisfying hobby than computer games! But if you don't succeed on this, use DVD track planning packages and train simulation recordings to widen their interest in the hobby.
- Undertake joint projects to introduce teenagers to various skills, eg: painting, application of transfers, weathering, etc.
- In this world of electronic gadgets introduce them to DCC as soon as they are ready. They will see that this can be just as interesting as the latest PC game!
- Show them the latest DCC sound locomotives and watch them smile!
- Use real trains on holidays and day trips rather than the family car. Not only is this the greener option but also it will convey the real life element of railways to the children.
- Join a model railway club if it is one where young people are encouraged to play an active role.
- Keep an eye out for manufacturer's new products targeted at different age groups. Manufacturers will be trying very hard to draw more enthusiasts into the hobby and to keep those ones already in the hobby!

A scene at Warley NEC Show 2007 with some very happy kids on the Underground Ernie demonstration layout.

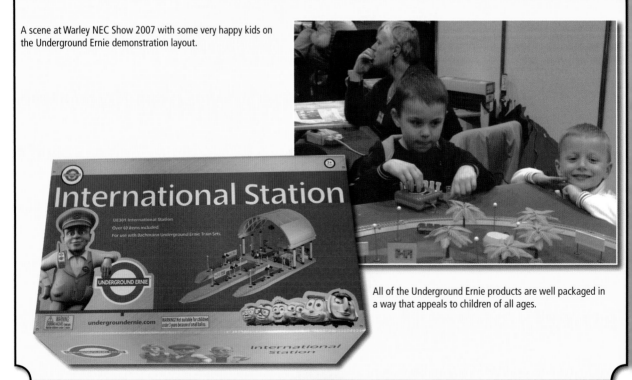

All of the Underground Ernie products are well packaged in a way that appeals to children of all ages.

Visiting preserved railway lines often provides the incentive to modellers to make a layout. We are blessed in the UK with a goodly number of these lines. The Severn Valley Railway operates between Kidderminster and Bridgnorth *via* Bewdley. One of the most picturesque stations on the line is at Arley, which is a small village on the River Severn. These pictures offer a brief survey of the station.

Preserved lines enable one to run steam and diesel motive power, as well as locomotives and rolling stock of different eras and railway companies together. So if you like to model various locomotive companies and both steam and diesel on the same layout, maybe you could consider modelling one of the preserved lines or making your own preserved line in miniature.

The station building has been well restored by the SVR and its many volunteers. Who could not be entranced by this classic setting?

Arley station, looking towards Bewdley.

Stanier 'Mogul' 2-6-0 42968 stands at the station on a Bridgnorth to Kidderminster service. All photos were taken in June 2006.

Left: Signal cabin. Note the details including the fire buckets, weeds between the rails, height of the trees, etc.
Right: Detail pictures such as this capture the constituent parts of a station. Here we see the gas lamp, fence, flower beds and stored freight rolling stock.

Passenger service calling at Meadfoot Bay Halt behind Bachmann Prairie tank.

GWR branchline in 4mm.

This compact layout is intended to depict a single line in Devon with a two siding goods yard. The buildings are limited to a goods shed and a halt. There are a few trees, a narrow lane to the goods yard and a small embankment running across the rear of the layout.

The track plan is loosely based on plan 33 in the Peco Setrack OO/HO Planbook (second edition).

The layout depicted would be

AIMS OF THE LAYOUT
- To build an OO gauge GWR halt using finescale track.
- To build a layout on one baseboard that is capable of being extended at both ends.
- To show a passenger station at its most basic.

suitable for someone making a 'long and thin' layout. It could be used initially with fiddle yards either end of the scenic baseboard, but the number of baseboards could be increased so that more scenic baseboards can be inserted between this layout board and the fiddle yard boards.

The buildings are from the new Bachmann Scenecraft range. These resin based ready-made buildings do make layout building a lot quicker than

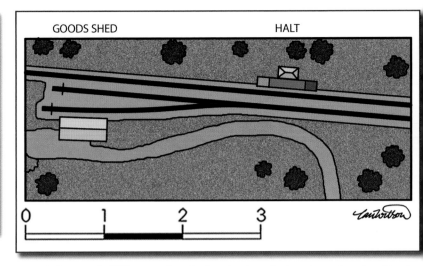

GOODS SHED   HALT

0   1   2   3

LAYOUT PROFILE

Size: 1.5 m x 0.60 m (5'0" x 2'0")
Country: UK
Location: A single branch line somewhere near the coast in Devon
Track: Peco Finescale Code 75
Control: H&M Duette
Scenics: Faller, Noch, Treemendus and Woodland Scenics
Trees: Noch and Heki
Buildings: Bachmann Scenecraft

using kits, though some would prefer to make their own buildings to individualise their layouts.

Scenically the layout is very simple. The green areas of the layout use scatter material sprinkled over PVA adhesive. Once the PVA has set a second layer of PVA was brushed across the scatter and Noch static grass was applied using a Noch Gras Master (see *BRM Book No. 2, Scenic Modelling* on how to use this tool).

The layout features some scenic details – Ratio telegraph poles, Hornby Skaledale milk churns, Bachmann Scenecraft people – but it would benefit from a lot more detailing. This would include road signs, fences, signals, yard lights, road vehicles, etc.

Pannier Tank in BR colours shunting in the yard

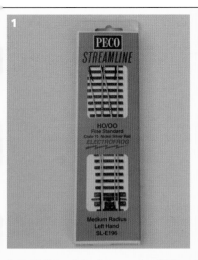

1. Peco's Finescale track was used on this layout. The rail is Code 75 which is a little finer than the Code 100 used in their Streamline Universal track range. The Code 75 track is suitable for locomotives and rolling stock with smaller wheel flanges. If you are in doubt as to whether your models are suitable for Code 75 either buy a sample point and piece of track to test run your models on, or stick with code 100 track.

2. Make sure that you use the correct fishplates when assembling the track! Here are the three different types sold by Peco for the Code 75, and Code 83 (for US style track) and Code 100 ranges.

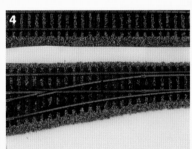

3. On this layout we used Gaugemaster's foam ballast inlay to represent ballast. The product is made by Noch and sold in the UK under stock number GM200. The rolls have fine stones embedded in the foam which is claimed to be very long lasting. The rolls are only sold as plain track so it is necessary to cut pieces to fit the points as shown in this picture.

4. The point on the layout with the Gaugemaster ballast roll fitted.

5. This view shows the entire layout as the scenic work was being developed. Note the simple track plan.

6. The Gaugemaster foam ballast inlay is easy to lay and looks realistic. **7.** The end of the sidings on the layout. The entire baseboard was painted after the track was laid. **8.** The goods shed is from the Bachmann Scenecraft range. I am not sure why the door is painted a light shade of purple!

9. I could not resist buying a private owner wagon from 1E Promotionals when I realised it carried my surname!

10. The halt is made up of two parts in the Bachmann Scenecraft range. The items are available separately – the platform and the pagoda hut.

11. Freight service passing Meadfoot Bay Halt.

12. Close up of the Halt. Whilst a platform such as this only accommodates one carriage, it is ideally suited to a GWR Autocoach, GWR Railcar or Class 121 single car DMU.

13. Well-dressed businessmen chat on the platform. These Bachmann Scenecraft figures depict the modern era, so perhaps Meadfoot Bay Halt should be on a preserved line after all!

14. Those gentlemen are now chatting to the engine driver.

15. 'Hullo, hullo, hullo'. Cameo comprising a policeman by Bachmann and Mini by Oxford Diecast.

Moving from easy model railways to finescale modelling
by **Ian Futers.**

08 718 shunting at Loch Lochy.

During the mid-1960s, when my interest in model railways led me away from the more usual oval of track into the realms of branch lines and more prototypical matters, the only track systems available were those offered by Tri-ang. At that time, I do believe Series 4 track had recently been introduced. Anyone modelling 'finescale' as it was then known, had to use perhaps the Peco spiked track system, or solder rail to small staples inserted into card or wood sleepers. A newer hand-built method, using copper clad sleepers, was also being tried out, but the most important revelation was the introduction of Peco Streamline flexible track. Yard lengths of this track were soon available, although it took an eternity for the small radius points to be introduced. When one looks at the Peco range nowadays, you can really only stand in awe at its magnitude. Of course, the modeller has many other track systems today, ranging from the diminutive Z gauge track up to the huge gauge 1 offerings.

I too commenced modelling with the new Peco Streamline trackwork, producing a large double track oval system, typical of the plans found in the modelling press during that period. It was a useful introduction into the world of flexible track, and you obviously had to learn how to make baseboards and then how to lay the track. Soft wood timber baseboards with the ubiquitous fibreboard surface and lots of Peco track pins! However, an important lesson was learnt in the art of cutting

Another early EM gauge layout Middleton North on the Wansbeck railway. J27 65860 is Nu-Cast kit as mentioned in the text.

Ian Futer's Top 10 Modelling tips

- Try and establish areas of interest within the country upon which you would like to base your layout.
- Then research to the best of your ability your chosen area.
- Commence layout building with a small and manageable project.
- Concentrate your spending on only what you require for your current project.
- Join a specialist society like the EM Gauge Society/ S4 Society/ N Gauge Society, etc.
- To learn more about your area of interest and join a specialist line society, eg: North British Railway Study Group.
- Have a go at scratch-building trackwork.
- Attempt some scratch-built buildings.
- Check out your local model railway club.
- Attend as many exhibitions as you can.

the track correctly and curving the flexible track sections, in order to allow a smooth transition at rail joints. Naturally the black art of soldering had to be mastered, as there were no such things as plug in electrical connections for the track and typically the basic electrical two-rail wiring practices had to be conquered.

After a while, I tired of running my trains in continuous circles, which were all basically ready-to-run offerings, because I had started to meet and talk with other railway modellers at a local model railway club. Individual travel was not really an option in those days, mainly due to lack of money, but I was becoming more aware of the national and local railway networks. I soon learnt that most of my model locomotives in particular, never actually ran in my own area and in any case, I was becoming more interested in the rural branch lines of Mid-Northumberland. The Tri-ang 'Britannia' would never have traversed such a line! I was reading about the histories of such lines and the companies that built them. It was obvious to me then that the trade would probably never offer the types of

locomotives and rolling stock that would have operated on such branch lines.

At the same time, the sharp radius of the readily available track systems did not suit what I was attempting to achieve. Side-by-side with this came the purchase of my first white metal kit, a Wills J39, which just happened to sit on a Tri-ang 0-6-0 chassis. After a while, the Tri-ang wheels were replaced with Romford driving wheels

The latest 'Futers' project 7mm scale "Victoria Park" an urban station set in Glasgow.

and new skills and techniques were attempted. All of the time, I was on a quite steep learning curve and numerous mistakes were made or encountered, but I knew I was striving for better track standards and running qualities. It was soon after the construction of Ashleigh, my seminal branch terminal, built in a week during 1972, that I started experimenting with copper-clad soldered trackwork in OO gauge. There then followed two West Highland based layouts in this gauge until about 1974, when I became a member of the EM Gauge Society and my modelling took its first stride towards the finescale aspects of the hobby in 4mm scale.

With the move to EM gauge standards, points were still constructed with copper clad sleepers. However, a

My final P4 layout, Newcastle Haymarket.

plastic flexible track was introduced in EM gauge by SMP and I constructed a number of small layouts based in the Borders. During the late 1960s, a series of articles appeared in the *Model Railway Constructor* relating to a new track and modelling standard in 4mm scale called Protofour. I had collected these articles and the links between EM gauge and the finer P4 standards were noted. The assorted items required to produce models in this finer scale were quite difficult to obtain, and supplies were erratic. Like many other modellers in the mid-1970s, I had the usual yard length of P4 test track along with two or three compensated wagons and vans, but no locomotives. Driving wheels with P4 tolerances were apparently difficult to manufacture, although eventually some types did appear.

My first layout to appear in this new scale of P4 was a Northumbrian branch terminus named Otterburn and it was to appear at quite a number of model railway exhibitions at the time. It was

operated with some of my old NBR locomotives made from GEM cast white metal kits. These locomotives had been originally OO gauge, then EM gauge and now they were P4 gauge and more to the point, operated within an uncompensated chassis, usually an old Tri-ang cast chassis block! I believe the care I took with my trackwork resulted

in the excellent running I somehow achieved on this layout. I enjoyed making the trackwork at this level and actually still do. Of course the P4 track was constructed using wooden sleepers with rail soldered to small rivets. Very time consuming, but extremely satisfying when you achieved the improved running qualities.

Lock Lochy station building, based on the one at Arisaig near Mallaig, scratch-built in 7mm scale.

Altaussee, my final attempt at an Austrian HO terminus.

I spent a number years working with the finer standards of P4 or 18.83mm gauge, which is the measurement between the rails of the track. Layouts such as Lochside, complete with modified ready-to-run diesels, were exhibited, and remember, there were no Bachmann or Heljan in those days! Other layouts included the huge Scotsgap Junction, a tiny terminus called Lochend, although I did take time off from P4 modelling to construct three HO scale layouts based upon Austrian prototypes. My final layout in P4 was Newcastle Haymarket and this small terminus can still be seen on the exhibition circuit today.

Wills J39 4813 at Saughtree, an early EM gauge layout and my first white metal kit as mentioned in the text.

I consider them to be quite basic principles, which can aid rather than hinder your approach to modelling. My first principle relates to knowing what area or region you prefer to model and then finding out as much as you can about that area. That includes historical details of the company that built the lines and perhaps their competitors. It follows that it is necessary to know which of the 'Big Four' companies operated the services after 1923 and then later still, what region it came under during the early British Railway periods. Obviously, if the lines you are interested in are still operational, you can go out and observe the prototype. Even if the lines have been closed, I consider it essential to try and visit

Nowadays I model in 7mm scale but still actually follow the principles I set down for myself way back in the 1970s.

specific locations in order to grasp the 'atmosphere' of the area. I consider atmosphere to be an extremely important issue when attempting to portray a particular scene on a model railway. Many of our regions had railway structures particular to that part of the country and frequently they had been there since the lines had opened in the 19th century.

All of the above information should assist you to only purchase items of rolling stock which relate to your chosen prototype. Of course there is nothing to stop you having more than one area of interest, I certainly research a number of areas which are of interest of me. This approach is an excellent way of attempting to keep your costs down to a minimum, unless you also

08718 shunts a fish van at 'Loch Lochy' (7mm).

An overall view of Loch Lochy in 7mm scale.

simply enjoy collecting models that appeal to you. It should also assist you to focus your attention onto your particular interest and heighten your awareness of its characteristics.

Another principle I try to follow is my approach to collecting not only locomotives, but also other items of rolling stock, such as coaches and special purpose goods vehicles. I really try to only use locomotives which I know have operated on my particular line, so therefore I go a step further and number my locomotives accordingly. This can be achieved from looking at old photographs, or better still actual records. The old locomotive shed books can also be helpful in pointing out classes of locomotive which operated in a particular region. Nowadays, locomotives, whether steam, diesel or electric, can very easily be renumbered with transfers and this creates individualism amongst your particular models. All too often you watch layouts at exhibitions and they seem to look much the same, which is a pity when you consider what the trade now offers. I could add that a modicum of weathering assists this individualism too.

I have mentioned that only using rolling stock distinctive to your area is an important step to achieving a more realistic model railway. Well, the same goes for model buildings too. It is highly unlikely any of the cardboard kit manufacturers or plaster cast building companies will ever produce a building, which suits many of the locations I have modelled. So I have invariably had to scratch-build any structures I have required from wood, card and plastic sheet. I have also had to use drawings or photographs of buildings in order to do this. For example, it is no good modelling the track plan of a particular Highland or Great Western Railway station, and then plonking a kit manufacturer's cardboard building of a nondescript station building on your platforms. Moving into the finer scale aspects of our hobby really does require some effort and research if your layout is to be remotely realistic to the eye.

The movement from 'train set' to 'finescale model railway' for me has taken a number of years and I consider it to be an ongoing process. Numerous skills and techniques have been learnt on the way and one needs to continually adapt and change methods and approaches. I started out working on small layouts, which were manageable for one person, to larger projects, which required a number of people to operate them. They say small is beautiful and that is something I have come to recognise in my modelling. By starting with a smallish project, it can be seen as an achievable aim. Too many large schemes fall by the wayside, the voice of experience is speaking here! A small layout need not be expensive, a larger layout definitely will be. Once you have grasped the basic skills of modelling, you may decide to concentrate on a bigger project. No harm in that, unless you fail to more-or-less complete the project, or worse still, lose interest in it. You could not do worse than follow the K I S S policies – Keep It Small Stupid and Keep It Simple Stupid! Whatever you do however – ENJOY!

Fort William in 7mm. 27 042 approaching the town signal box.

This main line station in Cornwall also features a designated platform for trains for the Looe branch.

The small station for trains to Looe stands at right angles to the double-track main line.

GWR colours in 2008! This is one of the signs on the platform for trains to Looe.

A classic sectional building still at use in the Network Rail yard.

Timber buildings still in regular use at Liskeard station, April 2008.

Platform building. This building would be ideal as a first attempt at scratch-building because of its simplicity.

First Great Western High Speed Train *en route* for London Paddington.

Even short trains can be interesting.
Here shunting takes place on
Pelle Søeborg's HO layout.

LARGE SCALE INSPIRATION FROM LENZ

As seen on their stand at the Nuremberg 2008 Toy Fair.

This O gauge demonstration layout shows what level of realism can be achieved in he larger scales.

Cameos like this can be featured on layouts in all scales.

Well laid track and some nice scenic work provide a good 'quality' feel to this layout.

	Problems	Possible remedies
LAYOUT DESIGN		
Accessibility problems.	Areas of the layout cannot be reached easily by hand.	At the planning stage consider how the tracks will be cleaned and how any derailments dealt with. Use detachable panels in the scenery if need be.
Storage yards are too deep.	Though a ladder of hidden sidings might look good on paper can the furthest siding be reached in reality?	Limit shelf-like storage yards to 18 inches unless they can be reached from both sides.
Moving the layout.	When it comes to the time to move the layout the realization comes that it will not be easy to move after all!	Planning a layout on paper is easy and fun. But think ahead for the maximum size of a baseboard that you can move comfortably (on your own) if necessary.
Why not start with a small layout?	Folks do begin railway modelling with rather grandiose plans!	Design the layout you'd really like then break it down into bite-size chunks. In that way you'll have the satisfaction of finishing each section.
You want two types of scene.	Many of us like more than one railway company or location.	If you are building a solid baseboard why not use a tall sky backdrop along the centre so that you can develop a different theme on each side of the sky?
TRACK		
Derailments.	Fishplates and rails have been fitted incorrectly.	Lay the track carefully. Try several locomotives on the track before it is fixed to the baseboard.
More derailments.	Do not always assume that the track is to blame.	Badly fitted wheels on any item of rolling stock. Sometimes the wheels have come adrift from their bearings.
A new locomotive derails.	It may be that it is not intended to go around the tight curves that you might have on your layout.	Many manufacturers specify that their locomotives should not be used on radii less than R2. Check with the manufacturer's instructions that come with the loco or look on their website.
Locomotives wheels touch the ballast.	Excessive ballast has been used.	If you are not too confident about ballasting the track use foam underlay or ready ballasted track. These might not look quite so good, but trains run well on them and they reduce the noise of passing trains.
Accidents occur in the most inconvenient places.	Carriages strike platform faces and tunnel entrances.	Test any newly laid track with your longest item of rolling stock before making any scenery. The same applies to the positioning of signals, fencing, huts and telegraph poles.
Dirty track.	Layouts do get dusty over time.	Use one of the many track-cleaning blocks on both rails. Use a fibre glass brush to clean the blades and adjacent rails of the points. Run a track cleaning wagon around the entire layout before each operating session.
Realism.	The moving trains do not look too realistic on the layout.	Maybe the curves are sharp – room constraints limit us sometimes. Use as gradual a radius as your baseboard will accommodate – for example use radius 3 and 4 rather than 2 and 3 if you can. Do not use 'S' bends on layouts (except with very gradual curves) – even a two-car DMU moving through 'S' bends looks ridiculous.

	Problems	Possible remedies
LOCOMOTIVES		
Jerky running of some locomotives.	Has the loco been stored for a long time?	Maybe it needs to be 'run in' again. Read the manufacturer's instructions.
Should we expect all locomotives to run beautifully?	Locomotives bought 20 years ago may look similar to the new one bought last week, but running qualities may be different.	Some older models never ran as well as today's generation of model locomotives. If you want the performance that is common today, consider if it is time to trade in your older stock for new models that might bring you more running satisfaction?
Keeping locomotives in good running order.	Has the locomotive been serviced recently?	Most manufacturers supply a lubrication guide with new locomotives. Do not over-oil but check that the loco is not running 'dry'.
SCENERY		
My scenery does not look as good as I would like it to be.	Some try too hard to make a scene realistic.	Go for a general landscape rather than a fully detailed one.
My layout does not look real.	The grass does not look the right colour and the trees look too small.	Study the prototype rather than working from the picture in your mind. You will be surprised how much there is to learn by looking carefully at real life and jotting down what you learn.
Surely making scenery should be easier than this!	Maybe you've not discovered the latest products.	The latest grass mats, foliage, trees, fences and other scenic accessories can be used to great effect and they are quick to use.
I want details on my layout but don't know how to start.	Detailed scenes seem more challenging than they need to be.	Let one of the manufacturers do it for you. Companies such as Noch and Woodland Scenics sell a range of different finished scenes complete with figures.
GENERAL		
I cannot build Kings Cross.	Most of us do not have the room for a huge station.	Join a model railway club and encourage them to see this as their next project! Revise your expectations – build just part of the station or build part as if it were off-scene. Try a smaller scale to work in.
Wanting to build a steam era line but not remembering what they looked like.	Possibly you were not born when steam was an every day occurrence. Even if you were, memories fade and sometimes are selective.	Engage in research. Join the appropriate society. Visit preserved lines. These are all fun and you can take the family along too.
Needing to improve model railway building skills before beginning work on a layout.	Sometimes when we enter the hobby our personal expectations are too high. We want to emulate a layout we saw at a show, tomorrow!	Build a compact layout to begin with. This will give experience across the range of skills required. Or speed up the process by getting a professional firm to build the baseboards and lay the track if you want to get on to scenery and operation.

This list is not intended to be exhaustive. It simply lists some of the possible causes of frustration for railway modellers. Usually the causes of frustration are relatively simple to fix. It is always best to review each day's progress on making a layout rather than jump ahead to the next stage. For example, test all newly laid track with a variety of locomotives and rolling stock.

APPENDIX

Recommended books for getting started.

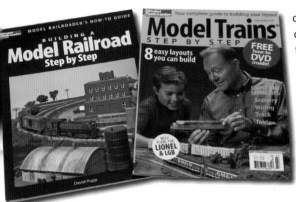

Model Railway Planning and Design Handbook - by Paul A Lunn, Neil Ripley, Ken Gibbons, Jack Burnard and Steve Flint. This excellent book features not only trackplans but also 3D drawings of finished projects. Some of the layouts are in the Easy to Build Layouts for Beginners category but others are more adventurous. The selection of plans caters for most tastes. This good quality production is inspirational for new and older established modellers. Some of the plans contain a track and scenic inventory listing all the products that can be used for buildings, fencing, trees etc on the suggested trackplans. This 96-page softback book is available from www.santona.co.uk

Building a Model Railroad Step by Step - this Kalmbach book has 112 pages, 250 colour photos and 20 illustrations. The author builds an N scale layout from scratch. There is extensive use of step-by-step photos and illustrations to give readers a chance to see all the techniques used

during a layout's construction. Whilst the layout depicted is a US one, the techniques and principles equally apply to layouts built in the UK. The chapters include planning the layout, building the baseboard, making scenery and operating the layout. In the UK, Model Junction and Steam Powered Video can supply the book.

Layout Designs for Operation - this 96-page book is by Atlantic Publishers. It explores ideas for developing a model railway layout with the emphasis on realistic operation. The two authors, Stephen Rabone and Trevor Ridley, discuss and illustrate this theme on both sides of the English Channel. The book contains eight designs in the United Kingdom, 10 in Europe and one in Jasper, Canada. Most designs are illustrated with photographs, a colourful trackplan and informative text. Some of the chapters are more comprehensive than others – for example, the Austrian station Semmering feature has a useful sidebar detailing the operations at the station. The trackplan sketches are a joy to study. Available www. atlanticpublishers.com

Peco's Setrack OO/HO Planbook - was updated in 2007. This is a very useful little book with 36 plans for the modeller to build, from tiny layouts to larger ones. The colour illustrations of

the plans are excellent. It was produced by two of the same team that brought us the *Model Railway Planning and Design Handbook* by Santona (mentioned above). It is a fun and practical little book that begins with a good summary of most of the basic constructional techniques than will be needed by the beginner. One of the best value little books available from www.peco-uk.com or any of their retailers.

Mountain to Desert: Building the HO Scale Daneville & Donner River - a softback book from the USA with 98 pages, with over 180 colour photographs and diagrams. The author Pele K Søeborg covers planning the layout, track laying, roads, building the landscape, water, trees, backscenes and the weathering of locomotives and rolling stock. Simply put, this volume is inspirational. Published in the US by Kalmbach, it is retailed in the UK by SPV and Model Junction.

NOCH Model Landscaping Guidebook - this 132-page A4 size publication covers all levels of expertise of layout building. Its 12 chapters include layout planning, baseboard construction, tunnels and bridges, rocks, water, landscape, vegetation, roads and detailing. The techniques described are arranged in order around the building of a compact European layout. Lots of stage by stage illustrations are included. Most of the techniques described can easily be transferred to UK layouts. All of the text is usefully in the English language. It is available from www. gaugemaster.co.uk

Modelling Scotland's Railways - by Ian Futers, is 112 pages with around 200 photographs and various colour sketches. It's a 'hands-on' guide on how to model Scottish Railways. There are also scale drawings of station buildings, signal cabins and more. The book includes both historical and current information to assist a layout builder. The prototype archive pictures and good quality photographs of a range of layouts all go to make up a very attractive but practical volume. It does show that a modeller concentrating on just one area in the UK can make a good variety of layouts. The book concludes with appendices highlighting areas of possible further research. Visit www.santona.co.uk

The Peco Setrack N Planbook was rewritten and produced in full colour in 2008. It is a useful booklet with over two dozen plans for the modeller to build, from tiny layouts to larger ones. As with the OO/HO Peco Planbook it was produced by two of the same team that worked on Santona's *Model Railway Planning and Design Handbook.* Available from www.peco-uk.com or any of their retailers.

Hornby OO Planbook – we should not forget the current issue of Hornby's long running planbooks. For more information see www.hornby.com

Model Railroader Planning Annuals – these are annual softback magazine style specials from the USA. The 2008 edition had 100 pages plus a free 16-page booklet. Each annual describes the building and design of over 10 layouts ranging from N to O gauges. There are more than 85 photographs – most of which are colour, but also some in classic black and white. I find that the words, pictures and features in these annuals to be stimulating. It is not simply a series of the normal descriptions of layout construction. There are 'planning tips' sections and throughout the publication

there are useful 'learning points' boxes. Do not be put off that these are US based publications – every UK modeller will find something in it of interest. Thoroughly recommended and good value. These magazines can be obtained in the UK at Model Junction or SPV.

Carl Arendt's Small Layout Scrapbooks - are presentations of numerous small-space layouts (less than 1200 x 1800mm). The books describe and illustrate in full colour small layout design, layout building and operation. There are several full-length 'how-to' articles, showing how to build compact layouts. In addition there are numerous modelling hints, tips and advice. If you think that you have no space for a model railway, you may consider that buying one of these books from the author at www.carendt.com is worthwhile.

Railway Modelling: the Realistic Way – this 352 page volume by Iain Rice published in early 2008 is useful for a modeller wanting to go to the next stage in railway modelling. The book is weak on the basic model railway construction techniques using ready-to-run equipment but is good for those folk wanting to move on to finescale modelling. Its publishers (www.haynes.co.uk) also retail a number of other useful railway modelling books.

Atlas planbooks – the US manufacturer Atlas produces products in N, HO and O gauge. They have a range of track plan booklets to go with their various track systems. In addition track planning software can be downloaded from their website at www.atlasrr. com

Peco 'Shows You How' booklets – these are useful small guides on specific topics. They are updated from time-to-time and cover a

range of topics including starting out in OO gauge, baseboard construction, tracklaying, DCC, scenery and more. Economically priced from www.peco-uk.com

Magazine supplements – from time to time most of the mainstream railway modelling magazines, eg: *British Railway Modelling, Model Rail, Model Railroader* etc. provide free supplements which are intended to provide a current summary of how to get into the hobby. These are worth looking out for because they are usually updated and discuss the latest trends.

Kalmbach planbooks and 'How To' books – this US publisher produces a wide range of model railway books including building a whole model railway layout in a variety of scales. Whilst not all of these would be suitable for UK type layouts, it is always worth looking at different ways of designing layouts to come up with a plan that really suits your wants. The construction processes described are much the same as for UK layouts. These books can be obtained in the UK at Model Junction or SPV.

Light Railway Designs and other Wild Swan books – whilst these may have a more limited audience, these slim publications nicely describe both the prototypes and the suggested layouts. The books include: *Modelling the GWR, Making Model Buildings,* etc. These are available from www.kevinrobertsonbooks.co.uk

A few final reminders.

Bachmann Scenecraft provender store

Buy a few of the main catalogues, eg: Bachmann, Dapol, Graham Farish, Heljan and Hornby to see the wide range of products that are available today.

- Visit a model railway show and see what appeals to you most. Is it scenic layouts, tail chasing layouts, historical or current image layouts?

Choose the era that appeals to you most.

- Decide whether you wish to model a specific location or an imaginary one.

- Buy some model railway magazines to read the accounts of other layout builders and study the magazine adverts for current prices of track, locomotives, carriages, etc.

- Consider joining your local model railway club.

- Choose the best place for a model railway in your home – permanent or temporary.

- Measure the dimensions that you have available for a model railway (including storage sidings).

- Make a quick sketch of the available

baseboard area. Remember, do not make the baseboards so deep so that access is difficult.

- Decide how much you are willing to spend on a model railway layout in a year – this might, for example, limit the track that you will buy to get your layout up and running initially.

- Draw up a few sketches of possible track plans. Do not be to tempted to fill the entire baseboard area with track.

- Think about the time that you can spend on your model railway in a year.

- We've all made mistakes. Most of them can quickly be remedied.

(This list cannot hope to be complete, or in the same order that all of us think is important. All of us are very different people. What is important to David might not be important to John. This list is simply an aide-memoire to some of the main considerations in building a first layout stage by stage).

- You might decide that it's better to build a layout in bite-sized chunks rather than see it as one large project – modellers usually gain more satisfaction over projects that are finished within a reasonable time, rather than large projects that may never be finished.
- Consider building a compact layout to begin with, even if you do have much more space available. You can learn a wide range of skills on one small layout. The compact layout could be altered to form part of a later larger layout.
- Use sectional track to build self-confidence in tracklaying. Test the track thoroughly before fixing it to the baseboard.
- Use ready-ballasted track and foam underlay so that you get some trains running – the quicker that you can run trains the more likely you are to stay in the hobby!
- Work out what scenery is right for your layout – use Learning Kits (eg: Woodland Scenics) to build up your scenery making skills.
- Buy a few ready-made buildings (Hornby Skaledale or Bachmann

Scenecraft) to give yourself a head start in giving the layout some scenic appearance.
- Do not neglect grass mats – these can be used as the base colour for level ground, embankments, etc. They can be fully scenically treated over time.
- Continue attending model railway exhibitions and reading books and magazines. Ask layout operators at shows, 'How did you make that?'

INDEX

Model Railways the easy way

CONCLUSION

In conclusion, I hope that this slim volume has given you a few more ideas for your next layout. Whilst I am aware that the products used on the layouts in the book are mainly of the 'ready-to-run' variety, this has been because these products are readily available and easy to use. The book has been prepared with both beginners and returnees to the hobby in mind and we have suggested these products so that building a first layout may be as enjoyable as possible. If folks enjoy their first modelling experience they will remain in the hobby.

Within the scope of this book I am conscious that we have not been able to cover all topics. Those that immediately spring to mind are: signals, DCC control, wiring, point control, building the baseboard and many more.

I have been a fan of Ian Futers' layouts for a rather long while. His 'small layouts are best' idea seemed to ring a bell in my mind too. With this in mind I approached Ian to see if he would be able to contribute a 'moving on from ready-to-run' chapter of the book. I am pleased to say that he said 'yes' and we can enjoy both his wisdom and pictures in this book.

My thanks also go to Pelle Søeborg of Denmark who contributed an inspirational picture in the book. To see more of his excellent work go to www.soeeborg.dk/railroading.html

Personal thanks go to Anthony Reeves, Dennis Lovett, Ian Fowler, Katrin Braun, Stewart and Farah Gorman, Laura Kolnoski, Tim Mulhall, Richard and Lynda Tebbutt, Mark Patrick, Steve Bird and Yvette Holler for their discussions and ideas as the book progressed.

I would also like to express my gratitude to those companies that assisted me during the production of the book. These included Atlas, Bachmann, Brawa, Dart Castings, Gaugemaster, Heki, International Models, Noch, Model Junction, On Tracks, The Model Tree Shop, Ten Commandments and Treemendus.

There are many more folk whose layout ideas have inspired me over the years. To all of you who build layouts that we can see in print or at exhibitions, thank you very much indeed.

The people at Warners need special mention – Jayne Thorpe who designed this book has been fun to work with. She has made the book look a lot better than I could ever do. Thanks also to John Emerson who initially approached me with the idea of writing a book for *BRM*. It had never occurred to me that I could, or should, write a book and here we are signing off on the second book. And to David Brown who sends me scenic prototype pictures with the request, 'Can you turn this into a layout by tea-time please?'

And my gratitude goes to you, the readers, for buying this book.

Finally, thanks to my wife Mary for putting up with layouts in most rooms of the house (at some times it felt like that even if, in reality, it was not true). Our vacuum cleaner has been worn out because of the amount of scatter materials and foliage it has picked up over the years!

AND FINALLY

Please remember:

- There has never been such a good time to participate in railway modelling
- Whatever you do in the hobby, enjoy it!